Dedication

I would like to dedicate this book to my children
Ashlyn, Taylor, Karsyn and Conley.
Dream big—anything is possible!

2 Hour House
Leadership from the Ground Up
is available at:

amazon.com

Target.com

Borders.com

Abebooks.com

Alibris.com

Booksurge.com

Also available:

2 Hour House motivational DVD

www.2hourhouse.com

TABLE OF CONTENTS

Acknowledgements

I would like to give special recognition to the following individuals who made the 2 Hour House a success.

To my wonderful wife for her encouragement and patience during the two-plus years it took to make this a reality.

To my father, Steve, for teaching me the values it takes to be a great husband, father and leader.

To the entire 2 Hour House Team for being an example of what a dedicated team working together in unison can accomplish. It never would have happened without everyone's involvement. Thank you all for your time and dedication.

To Brad Root and Carey Crist for their enormous time and dedication to this project.

To Jose Feliciano, CFP, for recognizing the leadership principles and life applications involved throughout this project and for inspiring me to write this book.

To Mary Ann Lackland for her desire to make this book a reality.

To Chuck Shinn for teaching me the organizational skills needed to coordinate such a massive undertaking.

To everyone who reads this book. I hope that our story will make a difference in what you do every day. It's not what we accomplish; it's the difference we make in someone's life that is rewarding.

To all the friendships created throughout this project. World Records will come and go, but the memories and friendships that the 2 Hour House created will last a lifetime.

Brian Conaway
June 2007

**Leadership from
the Ground Up**

Introduction

Something amazing happened on October 1, 2005. What was perceived as an impossible task, building a house in two hours, was in fact, actually achieved. Despite the skeptics, the challenges, and the extreme weather changes, 400-plus volunteering suppliers, friends and civic leaders joined me to fulfill this singular purpose that day. We met at a vacant lot in Tyler, Texas to build in record time, a 2,249 square foot home from the ground up.

What originally started as a lofty goal and charity fundraiser soon transformed into a life-altering, perspective-shifting phenomenon. The greatest outcome wasn't building a house in record time, it was creating a new way of thinking about building – everything. We built bridges between competitive suppliers and lifetime friendships with former acquaintances; we innovated industries and standardized convoluted construction processes. Equally significant, we discovered that a grand purpose pursued by inspired people could make anything possible.

We celebrated and cheered this feat, and all of us were forever changed because of it. Just when I thought it was over, my good friend Jose Feliciano proposed something equally daunting: take the 2 Hour House principles to people – everywhere.

"Brian," Jose pointed out, "What you learned from this experience about building a 2 Hour House should be shared with business people hungry to build richer lives and better businesses."

Jose's enthusiasm for taking what we learned and presenting it to entrepreneurs building dreams equaled my passion for building the 2 Hour House. It would take a lot of work to package this experience for executive training. I pointed out to Jose that I already operated a thriving home building company (www.conawayhomes.com) and that he ran a fast-growing wealth management firm (www.felicianofinancial.com). I added that we both had families and that it was just this side of crazy to start another enterprise, but he would not be swayed or deterred.

He was right: my 2 Hour House experience had little to do with a one-time record-breaking moment for the community and everything to do with forever altering business-building methodology. We could show entrepreneurial leaders how to defy the odds and build what others might perceive as impossible.

So, in late 2007, Jose and I co-founded the 2 Hour House company. The company is designed to reveal the proven eight-phase building process I refined from my experience, packaged with the proven business-building methods Jose developed with his clients over the last 15 years. The 2 Hour House membership-based training program provides the techniques and tools CEOs and spirited entrepreneurs need to build dreams beyond the imagination. We hope you enjoy our story (in this book) but we also hope you will check out our "building" the impossible membership program at www.2hourhouse.com.

Dream Big,
Brian Conaway
Jose Feliciano

I experienced the miracle from conception to birth. It was simply a match made in heaven. I had wanted our builders association to build a house that year. But Brian let me know he had a little bit larger plan...and so we did. And so we did.

Cherie' Paro

"The Granite Girl"

NOTHING IS IMPOSSIBLE

Nothing is impossible
if you believe it can happen

It was 4:30am.

I shoved my keys into my pocket that autumn morning and took a deep breath. The distinct smell of wet earth—fresh dew from the night before—filled my senses.

It was another typical East Texas morning. Cows meandered lazily in the nearby pasture while several horses snorted and stretched their stiff muscles. But this morning wasn't like any other morning.

No, this morning we were trying to set a world record. We were going to try to do something so unusual that it would question the impossible.

This morning, the world watched and waited.

Either we would prove the doubters wrong and go down in history. Or we would go up in flames.

Only time, the next few hours to be exact, would tell.

SETTING A RECORD

"What exactly did you want to do?" Whenever people ask me that, I have to stop and smile.

I remember when I first heard about a Home Builders Association in San Diego who had set a world record by building a traditional concrete slab house in less than three hours using standard building techniques. That record had stood unchallenged for over twenty years. I knew that I wanted to set a new record. My father had been in the home building industry all of my life and, at that time, I was serving in our local home builders association.

I wholeheartedly believed it could be done. And I knew we would be the ones to do it.

In fact, that's how I started out whenever I talked to anyone about my plans. "We're going to set a new world record. Want to be a part?"

Despite my candor, I realized immediately that this was the most challenging undertaking I'd ever encountered to that point in my professional life. And I also knew that it would likely be the most challenging project for 99% of the people I would need to help me accomplish it!

Still, it didn't take me long to get hooked on the idea.

The presenters at a Chuck Shinn management seminar showed some inspirational footage of how the San Diego team made history from the ground up. As I watched the video, I was intrigued.

Fascinated may be a better word.

Although the purpose of the film was to teach time management skills, I was concentrating on how innovations in the building industry could shave time off that world record. Despite the fact that building codes get more stringent every year, I knew that now, over twenty years later, it was definitely feasible to build an entire slab house in less than three hours. That's roughly the same time it takes to watch a college bowl game or play eighteen holes of golf.

I saw the possibilities. And I was excited. I couldn't wait to return home and start building momentum and enthusiasm for the idea among my colleagues. Traditionally, the president of our Tyler Area Home Builders Association (TABA) chose a project for the association to accomplish. In previous years, we had worked on various philanthropic projects, including a fire safety house my father had built in conjunction with the Tyler Fire Department that served as a traveling training and educational resource for children's fire safety. Another year, members of TABA had also donated materials and built cabins for a boys home.

At the time, I was the Secretary/Treasurer of TABA, and I knew that it would be a short two years before I became the president. I was already searching for something to do during my term that no one had ever done before. Something that would bring together the talents and resources our association represented among our 600-plus membership. So, when I heard about this world record from the eighties, it seemed to be the perfect fit for us in 2005.

By the time the inspirational footage was over and the lights came back on in the room, the ideas were flying through my mind. My first thought was, "What will my buddies (and fellow builders) Carey and Brad think about this idea?"

And the second was, "What will our dads say?"

In some ways, I didn't know what to expect from either one.

WANT TO SET A RECORD?

I first pitched the idea to my good friends and colleagues, Brad Root and Carey Crist. I wanted them on my team—they would be crucial to the success of the project. Brad and I had known each other since high school, and Carey was one of my most trusted friends in the business.

I knew they were used to my penchant for challenges, so I didn't hesitate to discuss my plans with them.

Playing video poker with Brad a while later on at a builders show in Las Vegas, I just put it out there. "Want to set a world record?"

I pretended to be intrigued with my poker screen at the same time as my question, letting it hang in the air for a good, long minute. Since we'd been friends so long, I could almost hear him thinking, "*Conaway, that guy…you never know what he's going to come up with next."*

But I was totally serious. And he knew it.

Before he could answer me, I started in. "When I become the President of the TABA, we're going to build a house from the ground up and do it in record time," I continued. "It's going to be a charity/fundraiser to draw our community together and see something they've never seen before. Want in?"

Brad, type A like me, was the first one to speak his support of the idea and gel with the general concepts I came up with later to get it done.

Carey, the more philosophical one among us, was a little more reserved when I sat down with him a few days later. I could tell it would take some time to win him over. In fact, by his own admission, he didn't even "get it" the first time I explained the full scope of the project.

> It was so out of the ordinary in our business to even consider all that would have to take place to pull this off.

It was so out of the ordinary in our business to even consider all that would have to take place to pull this off.

Setting up a concrete slab in twenty-two minutes when it usually took several hours to harden? Painting an entire house in less than ten minutes?

But, as Carey would later recall, it wasn't my grandiose plans that convinced him. I'd had time to prepare a basic flow chart and rough schedule by the time I talked to him. But he wasn't even all that impressed with the eloquent way I answered the questions he had. What helped him come around was my bedrock confidence that we could do it.

Carey recalled, "What hooked me, and I saw how it hooked other people, was the fact that Brian believed we could do it. He was so confident. I think when Brian proposed this idea to [other people], they didn't know exactly what hit them. He was obviously completely sold. He was closed. He was a Lay down Larry. And there was no talking him out of it."

Later, Brad recalled the moment this way. "At the onset, there was no doubt that we could do it." He added, "It was not a matter of, 'Could it be done?' It <u>had</u> been done. The question was could *we* do it and do it better?"

INITIAL PLANS

When I started this project, I immediately set three goals. First, this project would set a new world record, and it would take about 1000 workers and volunteers to accomplish tens of thousands of details in order to do it. Of that I was certain. Second, it would involve the builders association but also bring together the entire Tyler community, a growing city close to 100,000 people located two hours east of Dallas. Third, it would be a volunteer event to raise money for several local non-profits including Habitat for Humanity, Azleway Boys Ranch, a faith-based medical clinic called Bethesda Health Clinic, East Texas Food Bank, PATH (People Attempting to Help) and the American Red Cross. I knew we could get many of the materials donated in order to keep costs down. The home could be sold at market value and the money given to the non-profits. I hoped we could already have sold the house by the time it was built.

The founder of U.S. Steel, Charles Scwabb, once said, "You can succeed at almost anything for which you have unlimited enthusiasm." When it came to building what I began to term the 2 Hour House, my enthusiasm was out the roof.

I have always been a can-do guy. A dreamer. A thinker. But one who also gets it done. I never spend too much time with a dream before I start planning exactly what it will take to get there. Step by step, inch by inch. I envision where I want to go and then harness all of my energy to get there.

Maybe that's part of what made it difficult to understand why some of my colleagues tempered their response with trepidation when I told them about the idea.

After securing my friends, Brad and Carey, my next stop was convincing the Board of Directors for TABA to sign on to the project. Their first reaction to my proposal was the same as anyone who initially heard about the idea. They said, "You're crazy. That's impossible to do."

I just kept talking.

I talked to them about my three goals and made it clear that there were several other benefits to this kind of project. It would capture local attention for sure, but something like this could reach statewide and national recognition as well. In that sense, we could be an example for other home builders associations in our philanthropic tradition and really showcase what the home building industry was all about.

Something drew them about the brash idea; after all, human beings live for a challenge. But the same things that attracted them were probably the same things that made them extremely nervous.

Was it really possible to trim what was a typical 120-day endeavor (and that was working fast with no changes or delays) into a matter of mere hours? Nothing would be pre-built or pre-assembled. It would take months, even years, to get ready for it. How would we cover the thousands of tiny details? And get several hundred workers lined up to execute them? And who would do all of that—for free?

It must have sounded daunting. Whatever fears I'd had at the beginning, I was already over it by the time I started explaining it and drumming up support. But that wild-eyed look in their faces when I initially sprung the idea on them...that *worried* me a little. At least it gave me pause.

Was I crazy to think like this?

Was it really worth attempting (even with the distinct possibility that we could fail)?

I wouldn't know until I tried.

YOU GOTTA BELIEVE

"You gotta believe" was the catchphrase of New York Mets relief pitcher Tug McGraw in 1973. The Mets had come from far behind in a crowded field to win the division and the National League pennant.

Honestly, there were times during the next 18 months that "belief" was all we had. I believed it could happen, and I tried to transfer this hope into the other people around me. The Board eventually approved my idea to build a three-bedroom, two-bath, 2,249 square foot two-car garage home in less than three hours. I knew it was up to me to show them how serious I was about the project and begin putting details and plans in place. We scheduled the date of the build almost two years in advance for October of 2005.

PLANS CALLED FOR 2,249 SQUARE FEET, WITH THREE-BEDROOMS, TWO-BATHS AND A TWO-CAR GARAGE.

During the first few weeks after the Board approved the project, I scheduled initial planning sessions with Brad and Carey and left each meeting with even greater momentum fueling my steps. We'd been friends for many years, and I think we all knew that if one of us was going to undertake a challenge, we'd want the others to be right there beside us. Win or lose.

Our dads, however, were a different story.

DADS WEIGH IN

"You're going to get someone killed."

That was Brad's father's initial reaction when I tossed the idea his way. Brad's father, a successful high-end luxury home builder, did not mince words.

Even when Brad tried to counter with, "Yeah, Dad, but doesn't it sound neat?" he met with fatherly resistance.

"Sure," his dad responded with a glimmer of interest. "But

why would you want to do something like that?"

And then he returned to the line that would ring in our ears for months: "You're going to get somebody killed."

We laugh about it now, but deep down we all respected what his dad said at the time. His support of our endeavor would mean a lot—he was older and more experienced than any of us put together. My father, the retired CEO of our home building company, warned me that I had taken on an extremely large goal (which he knew would make me want to do it that much more!). He had been my mentor for all these years, and yet he wasn't entirely sure at this point that I hadn't lost my marbles somewhere along the way.

> "You're going to get somebody killed."

Fortunately, our dads did eventually warm up to the idea and gave us their full support. However, there were plenty of others who remained unconvinced. It would take some major selling on my part to get people to sign on to something of this magnitude.

One thing about me you have to know from the onset is that I never let up. I never give up. I could deal with a little objection or even an outright naysayer more easily than I could accept the slightest doubt in my own heart and mind.

There just wasn't room.

Ralph Waldo Emerson once said, "Nothing great was ever achieved without enthusiasm." I didn't just want to do something good for our community by raising some money. I wanted to do something great. I wanted to break the tape and reach the finish line on a project that would require everything I had to give.

And I didn't want anyone on the team who didn't want it as passionately as I did.

HANDLING THE CRITICS

Theodore Roosevelt once gave a speech on citizenship at the University of Paris in 1910 and included his feelings on critics. He said:

"It's not the critic who counts, not the man
who points out how the strong man stumbled, or
when the doer of deeds could have done better.
The credit belongs to the man who is actually
in the arena; whose face is marred by dust and
sweat and blood; who strives valiantly; who errs
and comes short again and again; who knows
the great enthusiasms, the great devotions and
spends himself in a worthy cause; who at the
best, knows in the end the triumph of high
achievement; and who at the worst if he fails, at
least fails while daring greatly, so that his place
shall never be with those cold and timid souls
who know neither victory or defeat."

I don't know what it is about human nature, but some people
don't want you to attempt something extraordinary with your
life. They are much more comfortable meeting the status quo day
after day; the impossible is just too threatening. So, if you begin
to move beyond the acceptable average, they want to drag you
down and your dreams, too.

It's not that I didn't expect objections. In anything you do in
life, especially something daring and out of the box, there *will*
be critics. You just can't let them distract you from your goals or
derail your intentions.

In this process, I found that anticipating objections is a
successful way to deal with the critics and move forward. The
best thing I could do to ward off the critics involved three facts:
1) There will be doubters; 2) They will have tough questions;
and 3) It's best to anticipate what those top questions will be and
have airtight answers.

In my mind, I tried to see a doubter as just another potential
supporter who needed more of the right information. I was
convinced that once the information was communicated to them
in the right way, they would either support us wholeheartedly or
they weren't the best fit for the team.

For instance, one of the examples I often used to explain how an entire house could be built in less than three hours was the sheetrock. Under normal circumstances, two people can hang one piece of sheetrock in a minute. Let's say that every person we assigned to sheetrock the house hung four sheets each. If we had enough people working in a highly organized manner, we could hang the entire house in record time. And I proposed that we would do it this way for every stud, window, piece of trim, light switch and doorstop.

When I explained it like this, people began to see the possibilities. It was exciting to watch their reaction! We took the simple approach that having enough people in the right spots doing the right things the right way could actually make this happen.

This philosophy formed the beginning stages of an enormous schedule and flow chart that identified every step to build a house from the ground up. We counted every second; and every second counted.

What about the ones who didn't understand or support our plan? Well, we had to move forward with or without them. The difference between a potential supporter and a critic is that a critic does not want to be confused with the facts. Their mind is made up. It is not worth your energy to address every question the critics may have. However, with a potential supporter, your careful preparation and presentation of the facts will make all the difference in the world.

> **It is not worth your energy to address every question the critics may have.**

Interestingly, through this process I also learned that just because someone says they will support your endeavor (and even invests time and energy into it), it doesn't really mean they believe in it like you do. And that's okay. Keep moving.

I met many people throughout this process who didn't really believe it could be done but they supported us anyway! They were involved, but their hearts weren't really committed. Like children at the pool on the first day of summer, they stuck their big toe in the water to test it. However, the vast majority of people who worked on the 2 Hour House were just the opposite. They were doing half-gainers and cannonballs off the diving board before they were even sure there was water in the pool!

TRUTH IN CRITICISM

I heard what the doubters, criticizers and opposition had to say, and I even listened for a kernel of truth in it to see if I was off base. For example, when Brad's father initially painted a picture of mass chaos leading to massive injuries, safety became an even higher priority in our minds.

We had to ask ourselves a specific question early on, "Was there potential for injury in this undertaking?" With a 30,000 pound roof section hanging in the air by the arm of a crane and a thousand people milling nearby, the answer was "yes." Definitely.

I have a friend who points out that we have "two ears and one mouth for a reason." In other words, we ought to listen twice as much as we talk. Do you listen for the caution in every criticism? We did, and then we discussed whether or not the caution was valid.

Sometimes it was obvious that we should blow it off and forget it. But other times we had to ask, "Was there a truth to apply? A lesson to learn? A base to cover?" We didn't let any critique go to waste...we shrugged off what was dispensable criticism and held onto whatever improvements we could make. In this way, we made it so that even our opponents helped us tighten up and get better.

These categories represented three pressing questions for which we knew we had to have answers. Our potential supporters (again, my definition for a doubter) wanted to know three things. How did we plan to have the concrete set up in 22 minutes? How could we tape and bed all of the sheetrock in the home in less than 15 minutes? How would we paint wall-to-wall in less than 10 minutes?

According to Brad, the answers to those questions were the key to securing early buy in. "When we realized we *could* do [those three things], we knew we could communicate how to do it to the people we needed buy in from…it opened their eyes and pushed them out of the box." We answered their questions by designing a system that would pull it off in record time.

(And as it turned out, 10 minutes was more than enough time to paint the house!)

THE BIG QUESTION: HOW?

From the beginning, it became obvious that even the most talented workers, engineers and sub-contractors were not going to build this house in record time. We could not point to a crack team of painters or contractors to address all the questions sufficiently. We would have to have something more.

Certainly, our plan was to have top quality people on our team; but we had no expectations that they were going to build this house in less than three hours by themselves.

No way.

We knew this house would be built in world record time not by the best human effort, but only if we had a system in place. Clever people would not build it, although we had the most talented people on task; only a foolproof system would. Therefore, we set our sights on designing a no-fail plan for every detail surrounding the project. I didn't even care who was going to do what…I would worry about that later. I mainly wanted to know everything I could about what was involved, and then I knew we could put people into action, tackling it piece by piece.

We spent two years developing a process to include every stick of wood, sheet of drywall and drop of paint that would come into the house. We knew where it would go, when it would go there and exactly how much time it would take to do it.

And then we assigned a person to every piece. The result was far beyond what several hundred volunteers could imagine… even with all of their best talents combined.

You see, the system clocked in early and stayed late. It worked rain or shine. It didn't grow weary or need to sleep in, even after two solid years of planning. The system needed to run on its own, once the clock started on the day of the 2 Hour House. There would be no time to pull out the plans and blueprints to see what to do next. The system that we designed set the new world record and it allowed all of us to celebrate.

I didn't even care who was going to do what… I would worry about that later.

A SYSTEM TO BUILD A HOUSE

Which brings me back to the morning of October 1, 2005. We chose to stage our production on three adjoining lots in a developing subdivision because no other houses were around it. We could park trucks, build a 2,000-seat grandstand and not worry about crowding in on the neighbors' houses. We had completed a practice house two weeks earlier (which was a total disaster…more on that later), and now the morning had finally arrived.

It seemed like a dream…I remember how the dawn crept up on the horizon and one million thoughts jockeyed for position in my mind, vying for my attention.

Snapshots of the last of the flow charts and production schedules panned by…only to be interrupted by one, pressing thought. Something most everyone there that day had on their mind: the concrete. Would it really harden enough to build on it in only 22 minutes?

Suddenly, headlights sliced the darkness wide open. One after the other, caravans of heavy equipment trucks, big rigs, vans and carloads of people began to arrive. And an endless parade of pick ups.

It was time.

To Think About

- What is your dream?

- What would you be doing right now with your life if you could do anything in the world?

- Who has told you it can't be done?

- Who would support you in this dream?

- How would your dream benefit others?

NOTES

I saw a form of organization that I'd never seen before. Presenting my team with a task and continually brainstorming the elements brought us to a clear understanding of what role each person would play. All of the puzzle pieces were not always available to us. Instead, we had to make the puzzle and then find all of the pieces!

Chris Baker
Chairman
Electrical Team Committee

A PLAN THAT WORKS

To accomplish your biggest dream, learn to build it backwards

D o you have a dream? Is there something you want to accomplish that is so intriguing to you that you stay awake at night thinking about it? Imagining what it would be like to see that dream come to fruition?

One thing I learned as this story unfolded was that conventional methods would not get me where I wanted to be. Although I had been in the building industry almost my entire adult life, I could not lean on standard building techniques if we were going to set a world record.

It would take something new…something I couldn't even envision at the time. New techniques, standards and products that didn't even exist would have to be developed.

As I said in the previous chapter, with a massive dream like ours, it takes a well-developed system and other resources to run the system—in order to be successful. And sometimes, that means building and running the system in an unconventional manner.

So many things that we ended up doing to build this house were essentially done backwards. Rarely was anything done in its typical order. For example, we planned to build the roof section completely separate from the frame of the house. We envisioned it would be constructed in one piece with all the plumbing and HVAC equipment dangling from the ceiling before we hoisted it above the house—as if we were placing the last tier on a wedding cake.

We had to *act* backwards, but we also had to *think* backwards.

If you recall the last time you drove through a developing subdivision, you've likely never seen the house frame going up with the roof assembly next to it on the same lot!

However, this allowed us to pour the maximum manpower onto the roof section without having to get in the way of those working inside the home. We were very creative throughout the process of finishing out the roof before we ever strapped it to a crane and gingerly topped the frame of the house.

We had to *act* backwards, but we also had to *think* backwards. Whenever we gained new team members, we told them about the project by starting with the end goal and working backwards from there. The goal never changed—we had to set a world record. From there, we worked backwards to lay tracks that led to its success.

Thinking backwards like this is a unique discipline that forces you to walk through proposed plans of action with a different perspective. For us, it meant starting most strategy sessions with a very important question: "What if?"

What if we did it this way? *What if* we tried it that way? We knew that if we did the same tasks essential to building a house in the same way that people were used to doing them, we would never make the record. That reality was clear. However, asking the "what if" questions brought us into the realm of possibility where no idea was too ridiculous. And sometimes the ridiculous was exactly the route we chose.

What if, for example, we laid carpet first and *then* trimmed the entire house after the carpet was laid? We could save a ton of time because we did not have to account for the sometimes tedious task of folding and manipulating the carpet under the baseboards. The baseboards would come in after the carpet and fit on top. That was something ordinary builders would never do.

But there was little that was ordinary about this project.

When it came to planning, convention went out the window. Experimentation was in.

COORDINATING THE CHAOS

My dad taught me an important truth about the home building industry. He said, "Any house is as good as the plan you start with."

The 2 Hour House was accomplished in less than three hours, but the planning took more than two years and about 1000 volunteers along the way.

I still have multiple three-ring notebooks filled to capacity with flow charts, critical path diagrams and meeting summaries. To find out how and why we were successful in the 2 Hour House, you have to look there first.

Within these pages, every nail,

EVERY DETAIL OF THE HOUSE HAD TO BE EXECUTED FLAWLESSLY.

© Conaway Homes, 2004

screw, bracket and truss is outlined and detailed. As the leader, it was my job to ensure every detail of the house was covered. I used a fair share of sticky notes accounting for each detail so that I could play with the order in which I thought it could be accomplished.

The system we built around this project was the result of thousands of hours logged by a team of talented men and women who were dedicated to making sure every last detail of the project was executed flawlessly—right down to the last electrical outlet on the last wall.

Early on, we created a chain of command. Carey, Brad and I formed the Executive Team responsible for all the major areas of the operation. We then divided the tasks into several broad areas and took responsibility based on our level of expertise and interest.

Brad, for example, was over roof, trusses and engineering. What do you get when a former CPA goes into the building industry? You get a very methodical planner with an eye for detail—that is Brad.

Carey has a background in hotel management and brought his people skills into play as he managed all of the safety issues and floated over many other areas of concern. Carey is such a likable guy—not only could he could sell a refrigerator to an Eskimo, but he could help keep 1000 people happy and focused on the task at hand.

I was over scheduling and the flowchart. Enlisting enough people, better yet enough of the *right* people, to be on our team was a critical step. I felt that I had the two best leaders in Carey and Brad to supervise the main divisions of the project. Now it was up to us to continue enlisting the next level of leadership in our organization chart.

We formed what we called the Quality Council from over two dozen TABA leaders and other individuals. Their job was to oversee a specific area of the building process within those three major areas and enlist people for that task force.

If something was needed to build the home, we assigned a

task force name to it. We listed areas like Plans & Specifications, Plumbing, Roofing, Framing, Electrical, HVAC (Heating/Ventilation/Air Conditioning), Insulation, Trim, Paint, Hardware and Tape & Bed.

We had an entire task force on Counter Tops, one devoted to Flooring, another on Materials Coordination/Staging and another singularly focused on Landscaping. Some of the not so glamorous, but necessary, task forces included Dumpsters, Portable Toilets, Volunteers and Food & Beverage. (However, coordinating toilets for over 3000 workers, volunteers and spectators on site the day of the 2 Hour House was an *essential* task!)

Each of those areas required dozens and sometimes hundreds of workers and tradespeople to develop the fastest, most productive way to execute the responsibilities for that task. Each Quality Council member was responsible for communicating with and motivating his or her tradespeople and workers as the Chairperson of that task force—not always an easy job.

We also included a representative from the Tyler City Inspections Department, Renee Bennett, city of Tyler chief building official. She served on the Quality Council and attended all the meetings, making sure everything we were planning to do would meet or exceed standard building codes. It was important to me to build a quality home that would be move-in ready, even though we would be constructing the home in less time than it takes to move in!

MEETINGS, MEETINGS, MEETINGS

With about 18 months until October 1, 2005, the Quality Council began meeting once a month. Soon, we realized that we would have to double, then more than triple, the frequency of these meetings. The various members of the Quality Council met at least once a week, and sometimes several times a week, to discuss everything in detail. Toward the end, there were days that it was not unusual for me to attend eight critical meetings.

And I did not attend every meeting! I purposefully stayed out of many meetings because I had to convey full confidence in my leaders. If I showed up at every meeting, I would overshadow my leaders' authority and everyone would be looking to me for answers to their questions. I wanted to be able to hand over the responsibilities to a leader in whom I had confidence and trust that the job would get done.

Whenever there was an issue, each Chairperson would hopefully be able to address it directly before it became a problem for the whole Council to discuss. However, there were certain times that the entire Council did have to discuss a specific concern in detail, such as painting, drywall and tape and bed, and vote on it.

For example, we examined all the ways we could do the trim in the house. We could nail it. Or we could glue it with one of the many fast-setting types of glues available on the market. However, it wasn't a matter of simply choosing which would work best for the trim. Because everything had to be done in a certain order, we had to consider how one task would affect the one that came after it.

In the case of the trim, if we glued it and the glue wasn't dry by the time the carpet guys came in, they would knock it off the walls. (This is another reason why we decided to go the non-traditional route and install the carpet first and then *nail* the trim on top of the carpet!)

Although the Chairperson may have been recognized as the expert in that field, the various areas involved in building a house overlapped so much that talking about certain issues together was necessary. The task force would come to us with a recommendation or an item for discussion, and we would all weigh in on the issue.

"WHAT DID I COMMIT TO DO?"

By their own testimony, many of the leaders on the Quality Council agreed to the project before they understood exactly what they were committing to do! I don't think many of them fully understood the magnitude of their role in the operation and the amount of time, energy and resources it would require over the next year and a half.

Dick Schilhab, vice-president of the concrete company we selected, agreed early on to lead the challenge of developing a quick-drying, self-leveling concrete that would have to set up in roughly 22 minutes.

However, it wasn't until later that it dawned on him what he had agreed to do!

Dick recalls, "I told him that we could do it, but I had no idea what I'd agreed to. It was so far away [in the calendar year] that it was easier to say you would do it. Finally, it began to get closer to the time when we needed [to begin research] and I realized we really were going to do this thing."

> "I told him that we could do it, but I had no idea what I'd agreed to."

To understand the scope of the challenge, it's helpful to understand the typical slab process. Typically, a concrete crew pours a house slab over the course of two to three hours. The finishers let it set for four to five hours after they have raked it into the forms. Overall, it is usually a ten-hour process before anyone attempts to even walk on it, certainly not build on it. The building process does not begin until the slab has gone through its initial set and has reached what is called a "hard set." It then goes through several strength gains over the next few days before it is ready to accept the framing, roof, etc. That's just how it's done.

Dick remembers meeting with his area operations manager in January of 2005 to set goals for the year. You can imagine the look on his manager's face when Dick told him that one of his goals was to get ready to pour concrete in the fall that would harden fast enough for a house to be built on it in about 22 minutes!

His next meeting was with one of his primary chemical

suppliers. When Dick explained what he needed, "he basically fell over dead and said, 'You can't do that!'" Undeterred, Dick spoke with the engineers next. That's when he got his first glimmer of hope—from the engineering department of all places! They saw an interesting problem and were curious to begin solving it. The engineers in Cleveland, Ohio began researching mixes and tested them over the spring and summer, finally settling on a mix that would work.

In addition to the concrete, companies from all over the nation were testing and researching various techniques and materials, some of which were developed exclusively for the 2 Hour House project.

> If there was a faster and better way to do something, we wanted to know about it.

If there was a faster and better way to do something, we wanted to know about it. And I wasn't shy about asking for other people's input. I remember being at a home builders' fish fry and talking with some associates about our project. One of the guys there owns a company that deals in custom storage solutions for closets, laundry room, garages, etc. I was talking to him about my need for a "quick closet-solution" to finish out our closets in the 2 Hour House. It wasn't long until my fish-fry buddy faxed me a photo and link for an expandable metal hang rod/shelf combination that might do the trick. It was so ingenious that we ended up using it for the project.

This kind of thing happened all the time as different people spread throughout the building industry put their heads together to come up with solutions for us to consider. I had business cards in every coat pocket and cubby hole in my truck for everything from hydraulic cranes to quick-dry mudding, to millwork cabinets, to electrical supply and even grandstands for our spectators!

Working with All Kinds of People

While the right materials were definitely an x-factor in our plan, the way we utilized people was also unconventional. My dad has been in the home building industry for over 30 years, and he has seen a lot of trends. One of the major obstacles he cautioned me about at the beginning of the project was what he saw as a difference in work ethic between today's workforce and that of the eighties when the world record was set. What if my workers wouldn't commit to a project like this? Worse yet, what if they committed to work, but didn't pull it off because they grew discouraged or disinterested?

Like many in his generation, he felt that the draft did a lot to hone a committed work ethic and discipline. "In my time, people showed up to work on time and did not take unnecessary breaks," he told me. "And when we did break, it was an exact break for [ten minutes] or so. There were thirty-minute lunches. There was no 'going off in your car' and leaving the site at noon."

I have other friends and colleagues who think changes in education have made a difference in lowering the expectations of today's workforce. There are probably several factors that have contributed to a less disciplined workforce culture over all. I know for a fact that this undertaking was the biggest professional challenge that most of the people who served on this project had undertaken to that point or ever would do in their lifetimes.

Would I be able to count on them? Could they count on each other to get it done? The answer was largely unknown.

Tradeworkers are notoriously come-and-go employees who float from job to job wherever there is a good-paying opportunity. They are also a pretty rough crowd to work with sometimes, and they are very competitive and territorial about their work. It wasn't an easy job for the Chairperson to coordinate this band of people, ranging in age from confident twenty-year-olds to seasoned senior adults. One of the biggest challenges in their job was selling the workers on the whole idea of thinking backwards.

For them, it meant thinking about how their work affects the person that comes after them in the building process—something they rarely have to do in a typical home. In other words, each trade group—foundation workers, framers, drywall people and painters—would have to work in much closer proximity than they typically have to do.

For example, a painter usually comes along well after a trim carpenter has completed his work. The painter almost always complains about how another trim carpenter trimmed the house.

The painting crew can never seem to understand why the trim carpenters don't observe certain considerations, however remote, that would make the painter's job infinitely easier. For the first time in a home building project, everyone involved in the 2 Hour House was in the same room at the same time—and sometimes they were stacked on top of each other trying to get their work done!

Although most of the conversations in the Quality Council were intense, overall they remained civil and productive. However, there wasn't always a pleasant exchange among the actual tradesmen on the scene, where egos got in the way and turf wars erupted.

I recall one disagreement on a test site between a painter and someone working with the drywall that almost went to blows. However, by the time the 2 Hour House project date rolled around, the various teams of workers who were usually fierce competitors learned to respect each other and work as a single unit, a team, side by side.

According to one leader, there were guys there that could not even sit together at the same lunch table before the 2 Hour House. Now, they were willing to set aside their competitive nature and focus on a common goal.

This was another "backwards" strategy that resulted in some surprising gains for our team. The overlap gave us the opportunity to talk about what special considerations each group could make to ensure the other group succeeded.

Which leads me to ask you this question: "What would happen in your organization if everyone was in the room at the same time?" In other words, are people working toward the same common goal or trying to protect their turf? A healthy organization means everyone appreciates the other members on the team and realizes their importance and value. A decision that may make things easier on myself but harder for someone else down the line is not a good decision for the team. The key is to think about a task from the perspective of everyone involved in the project—from those with the least responsibility to the greatest responsibility. Seeing the same task from all of those different angles can generate some innovations you would not understand or envision any other way.

> A decision that may make things easier on myself but harder for someone else down the line is not a good decision for the team.

FORGET EVERYTHING YOU KNOW

During our preparation and planning phase, we constantly turned the box upside down and said, "Forget everything you think you know about building houses."

Try it another way.

In that time, we tested hundreds of products and techniques that would increase the efficiency and workflow. We even invented several of our own. We used several homes in various stages of construction as test sites for various products. We could test a tape and bed product, for example, in the garage then go back and strip it all out after we made our findings. Several task forces would have their meetings at these test homes to demonstrate a product's performance or to time a particular task, such as hanging sheetrock in one room, to see how fast it could be done.

Another example of unconventional, time-saving thinking was that we planned to install plumbing in the sinks outside of the house before they were brought inside the house. Again, the less we needed to do inside the actual home, the better. We began by installing the sinks into the countertops, as well as the faucets and hardware. Several guys would simply hoist the lengthy countertops by hand, sinks, faucets and all, and walk them into the appropriate rooms—ready to install. Instant bathroom.

In a similar manner, we planned to install the hardware on all of the doors to save time, then bring them into the house and install them. In the plan we developed, we had accounted for every last knob, deadbolt and doorstop throughout the home.

When it came to establishing the walls of the home, we really had to do things in an unusual way. We decided to install the electrical components and wiring into the walls *before* setting them. Again, it was a matter of avoiding congestion inside the home and trying to think of every time-saving step possible. Section by section, we planned to lay out the wall studs and panels in the grass and attack each one with nailguns and wires.

I'm particularly proud of the way we arranged to finish out the walls by sheetrocking the interior walls first, then adding insulation, followed by siding—working our way from the inside out. Not at all your typical order.

However, in doing so, we knew we could shave off precious minutes. Finishing the interior walls first and working our way outward meant we could continuously throw scraps out the sides of the house instead of piling it up and hauling it out of the front and back doors.

Value engineering allowed us to save time in the way we designed the house. We did ourselves a favor by using limited, even-numbered cuts so that we did not waste time measuring with a pencil for complicated lengths involving sixteenths of an inch. Instead, we made simple, even cuts for the boards, trim, carpet and sheetrock.

We were looking for the minimum amount of labor, materials and time necessary to accomplish every task and often had to weigh the pros and cons of doing it one way over another. We had to account for all of the materials and decide ahead of time which materials would save the most time in assembly and installation, which posed some interesting dilemmas.

For example, a room that measures 10 feet 6 inches wide would waste a lot of sheetrock and require unnecessary cuts because sheetrock only comes in 8-feet, 10-feet and 12-feet sheets. We could narrow the room to ten feet wide. However, carpet only comes in certain widths, too, and narrowing the room might cause problems for the carpet laborers who want as few seams as possible.

Which one should we plan around? Would it make more sense for the sheetrock guys to make their cuts and have some waste? Or would it make more sense for the carpet guys to put a seam in the room? Nothing was left to chance. In this instance, we designed around the sheetrock because the fewer joints we had to seam together by taping and mudding, the more time we would save. We played out hundreds of similar scenarios in our minds, weighing the pros and cons in order to make the best decisions.

> We did not have half a day or even half an hour to waste.

Finally, we poured on the speed when we figured out a unique way to install the garage door. Believe it or not, it usually takes a team about three hours to install a garage door because of all the components, measuring, etc. We did not have half a day or even half an hour to waste.

Scheduling Everything on a Micro-timeline

We completely changed the master flow chart twenty times or more during the planning process, trying to keep it to one page. In contrast, when we refined the more detailed master schedule, it was over 22 pages long. The trick was that the contractors working on various areas of the house would have to commit the plans to memory because there would be no time to check them on the day of the event.

Amazingly, the master schedule captured every detail of 120 days worth of building a home into a micro-timeline of 2 hours, 43 minutes. Everything that needed to happen to produce the desired outcome was mapped out on paper.

To put it another way, imagine it in the context of a family. In a family, parents have 18 years to raise a child. Their goal is to pack in all of the lessons they can during this time about character and values so that their child grows up well-equipped to function in and contribute to society. But what if you only had 21 days to raise a child?

Overwhelming, right? It's a similar ratio to taking a typical 120-day schedule and reducing it to a number of hours. Yet in that limited timeframe we still did everything we needed to do to accomplish our goal of building a quality home.

If you only had 21 days to raise a child, what priorities would become clear? What crucial lessons and information would you want to make sure you passed on to him or her?

> What is unimportant is shoved to the background, and the most important aspects of your goals suddenly get your attention.

Hypothetically speaking, if you only had 21 days to create a foundation for a company that would outlast and outlive you, what would you want to make sure you did in those three weeks? Is your answer to that question on your desk right now and in your to-do list? Or are you focused on a myriad of distractions that are not that important to your overall goal?

When you create a hypothetical micro-timeline of a goal that you want to accomplish, priorities shift. What is unimportant is shoved to the background, and the most important aspects of your goals suddenly get your attention.

In our micro-timeline of a few hours, every second we saved or lost was important. As I'll explain later in the story, we lost about 15 minutes or so on the day of the event when we set the walls. That seemingly small delay would normally be nothing on a 120-day schedule. But every minute weighed so much more than a mere 60 seconds on a clock in this project. In a micro-timeline, fifteen minutes could have meant losing the record entirely.

This kind of perspective gave every person's task and responsibility, no matter how large or small, newfound meaning.

LASERBEAM FOCUS

In order to equip a tradesperson with the ability to focus with laserbeam accuracy on the one responsibility he had (and not be overwhelmed with the myriad of other details), I asked myself several questions. What would he need to know in order to do his job? What would need to be done before, during and after his arrival on the scene?

For some, their responsibility may have been a seemingly trivial task. One worker, for example, had the sole task to walk in the front door of the 2 Hour House, go to Bedroom B, Wall C and install a single outlet. Once he completed that task, he was to walk out the back door of the house and clear the field. His contribution was finished.

> When you put a system in place, even the most seemingly insignificant acts are rich with meaning.

And there were hundreds of others like him with similar jobs that they repeated all day.

Do you think that guy felt insignificant to the process? He could have felt that way. What does one single outlet matter in the greater scheme of an entire house anyway? And yet, if that single outlet did not meet code, the building inspectors could not have issued the certificate of occupancy and the whole project would have failed.

When you put a system in place, even the most seemingly insignificant acts are rich with meaning. We ensured that everyone involved in running the system understood their position in the plan and executed it to perfection.

We were able to shrink onto one sheet of paper an

abbreviated version of a critical path diagram showing all of the major tasks. In miniature type, we detailed four major groups representing over fifty essential tasks that would be happening simultaneously: Group 1-Foundation; Group 2-Wall Section; Group 3-Roof Section; and Group 4-Assembly (which included installing door hardware, attaching cabinets, prepping light fixtures, etc.). Each of those fifty-plus essential tasks broke down into several thousand miniature puzzle pieces that had to come together just so.

TIME VARIABLE

One of the variables in the puzzle was time. How much time would it take to perform each task? How much of the task could one person do? How much time would it save if we divided the tasks among several hundred people?

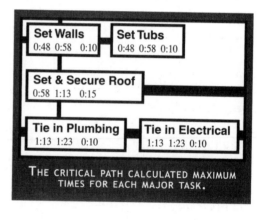

THE CRITICAL PATH CALCULATED MAXIMUM TIMES FOR EACH MAJOR TASK.

On our diagram, we assigned a start and finish time to every task. Take the front porch columns for example. Based on the number of people working on that one task, and the number of responsibilities required to complete it, I determined that we could squeeze everything necessary into a 10-minute timeframe.

We determined a maximum timeframe the plumbers would need to rough in the plumbing for the foundation. In lightning speed, they would have to dig the ditches, lay in the pipe, install a two-inch sleeve for water and refill the ditches. However, we had access to over 40 plumbers for the 2 Hour House. Working together, we estimated it would take them only seven minutes. However, the plumbers consistently out-performed our estimates and shaved time off the clock with every task.

Using this method, we determined that 15 minutes were

needed to insulate the attic; 30 minutes were needed to install the shingles, vents and boots; 10 minutes were needed to set the bathroom cabinets and doors, and so on. Because of the inordinate amount of manpower accessible to us, and the organized way in which they were utilized, we were able to shrink massive tasks that would usually take days into mere minutes.

That meant we could install vinyl flooring in the same time it takes to microwave a baked potato. Or lay carpet for an entire home in the time it takes to warm up your car on a winter's day. For the paint, we had set aside roughly enough time to take the dog for a 10-minute walk around the block, but we ended up painting the interior of the house much faster—in about the same time it takes to brush your teeth!

> We ended up painting the interior of the house much faster—in about the same time it takes to brush your teeth!

Smaller tasks that would require only a few team members to complete were calculated to the second. We even estimated five minutes were needed to install the mailbox and the small perimeter fence around the yard.

Doing it this way for every task, we estimated that we would build the house in exactly 2 hours and 43 minutes.

SEQUENCE MATTERS

Sequence was another variable in the puzzle. All of the steps had to be taken in a very specific, sequential order. For example, there were ten sets of essential tasks (each representing hundreds of steps) that had to happen to the roof section before we were ready to set and secure it. For example, the shingles had to be installed. It was the same with the foundation—four sets of essential tasks had to be completed before we could begin to set walls on it. And the walls required three sets of tasks before they could be set.

However, it had been designed it in such a way that many of these tasks would be happening simultaneously because of traffic flow and proximity—how close the task was happening in proximity to other tasks. In other words, what could we do at the same time without getting in someone else's way?

For instance, while we were installing the front porch columns, other crews could be connecting the roof to the main frame of the house. One crew would be able to install the plumbing, another could connect the electrical and still another could tie in the HVAC. At the same time that those tasks were happening, other crews would be installing the windows, another would be setting the exterior doors and still another would be caulking/insulating the bathrooms. All seven tasks would happen simultaneously, and believe it or not, we believed it was possible to do all of the above tasks all at once in 10 minutes flat.

I visualized the entire project this way. It was an enormous puzzle with thousands of interlocking pieces. But once we dumped everything out of the box and onto the lot that was nestled inside a new subdivision on October 1, would all of the pieces fit together?

> Simply gathering enthusiastic and talented people around you will not get you where you want to be.

No Substitute for Planning

In the process of learning to build my dream backwards, I became even more convinced that there really is no substitute for practice and planning if you want to see your dream become reality.

As much as I wanted to make this happen, it became clear that you cannot depend on the strength of your personality or personal fortitude to accomplish a dream this enormous. Those things will help and certainly add value. But they can't fuel a project far past the starting line if you haven't taken the time to plan or discipline yourself and your team to work your plan.

If you rely too much on your own ability, self-will and sheer determination to launch your dreams, I guarantee you will find yourself struggling with burn out somewhere soon down the road.

Likewise, simply gathering enthusiastic and talented people around you will not get you where you want to be either. I had hundreds of workers who were charged about the 2 Hour House project—they couldn't wait to storm the field that October morning.

However, unorganized, enthusiastic people cannot accomplish much of anything! In fact, they will more often make a mess of things as opposed to advancing your goals.

PRACTICE HOUSE

Two weeks before the scheduled 2 Hour House project, we executed a practice house—actually two practice houses. This would be a time to put all our preparation and products to the test and would give us real-time feedback on all our research and planning. Two teams would compete against each other for the best time, which would also give us the chance to choose the strongest participants to have on hand for the real event a few weeks later. The excitement and energy in anticipation of the practice day was intense.

Little did we know that all of our precious planning would soon prove to be utterly worthless as the day approached. Just before the practice house build, we lost our cranes and generators to a little lady named Katrina... but that was only the first of many bad omens. As the actual day of the practice house progressed, we realized we had our own disaster on our hands.

TO THINK ABOUT

- What does it mean to build a dream backwards?

- In what areas of your professional and personal life are you open to thinking outside the box? Why?

- In what areas are you hesitant to do so? Why?

- "Convention was out. Experimentation was in." What would happen if you approached a current problem you're facing with the question, "What if...?"

NOTES

What I learned came at the expense of failure! Our concrete team failed on several occasions while testing our trial batches. However, after many failures, we finally achieved success the day of the record-setting event.

Randy Humphrey
Chairman
Concrete Material Committee

PRACTICE MAKES PERFECT?

Learn from your mistakes
Don't repeat them

I felt like Thomas Edison, the inventor of the light bulb, who was asked early on about his lack of progress during the initial research phase of his invention. "I have not failed," Edison remarked to the reporters' inquiry. "I've just found 10,000 ways that won't work."

In preparation for the practice house, I had personally been onsite at dozens and dozens of tests regarding various building products. Practice took on a whole new meaning during the research phase because we had to search constantly for new ideas.

We made phone calls and scheduled meetings with various industries trying to crack the code on the kind of paint that would dry to the touch in minutes or a wall mud that wouldn't interfere with the drying process.

It was a while before we could even "practice" our techniques or products because first we had to settle on what would actually work. It wasn't a matter of finding the right product...sometimes it was a matter of inventing what didn't even yet exist. We spent a lot of time in the experimental phase doing just that: experimenting.

If it's been awhile since your organization spent some time just experimenting instead of always doing the same old thing, you might benefit from some designated out-of-the-box think time. Research a new trend. Creatively punch through the wall of a perplexing problem with some possible scenarios.

Dream together.

It's a good exercise for families, too, to try new activities and breathe new life into their routine. Sometimes we get in a rut and are so scared of trying a new way to structure our home lives that we never think creatively as a family.

The 2 Hour House project had its fair share of discovering thousands of things that wouldn't work, such as countless trial and error experiments with paint and texture products for the walls. There were several innovative products available to us, but the main concern was the drying time. We even located a product that would perform every step at one time—texture, paint, the whole thing. Only it took two hours to dry. We needed to paint the entire house in less than ten minutes. Above all, we tried to ask ourselves, "Would we want this product in our homes?" That helped us maintain an eye for quality, too.

Not only did the product need to be right, we also had to consider the traffic flow when that product was being used. What steps could be accomplished at the same time? What would have to wait? Where could the materials be staged while they were being used? Every decision brought with it a number of variables to sort through. However, once we discovered a winning formula or product or technique, we spent time honing it and perfecting its qualities through practice after practice.

None of the product tests was more fascinating to watch than the concrete experiments.

Depending on the mixture of the chemicals and the order in which the chemicals were mixed, Dick Schilhab and the guys he had working in the lab became sort of a flavor-of-the day ice-cream concrete operation. They could mix it fast or slow, with pecans or without.

Dick's goal was to have a concrete mix design by the end of April 2005. In mid-May, it still wasn't perfected. Dick recalls the instructions he gave his work crews. "I finally told my guys that they would just have to get out there and mix it up and see what works and what doesn't." That meant a lot of room for trial and error! The right mix had to be pretty fluid so it would flow out of the trucks and begin self-leveling, but it couldn't be too watery because water slows down the set.

In their experiments, they came up with several mix designs that they would test in the late afternoons. They built some forms on site and, according to Dick, "hired some finishers to see what they could do with a load of it."

They even brought in sand that would be similar to that on the actual site so that even the moisture content of the sand would be consistent with the real thing. Those 20 or so experimental batches would do amazing things—stuff people had never seen before. Soon, word spread that something was afoot at the plant as interest in the search for the perfect foundation piqued.

> Those 20 or so experimental batches would do amazing things—stuff people had never seen before.

As the summer of 2005 wore on, small crowds of industry leaders, workers and interested bystanders would come to witness test batches each week. People were fascinated by what they saw.

Some mixes would set up in as little as five minutes due to the special combination of chemicals and additives. That's barely enough time to get it out of the truck basin, down the chute and onto the ground before it hardens in a lump.

Don't believe it?

Just ask any of the several hundred people who were there the day we held our practice house competition when 48 cubic yards of concrete mix did just that.

PRACTICE DAY

On the day of the practice house, the weather was unseasonably warm. It had been over 80 degrees all week, and everyone was soaked through their shirts. Several weird things had happened recently with the weather during the fall of 2005, namely Hurricane Katrina a few weeks prior. (Locating cranes and generators in the middle of a national disaster like Hurricane Katrina is a story in itself that I will share later. Let's just say it wasn't easy.)

> The fourth most intense Atlantic hurricane ever recorded made landfall only a week before our record house would be constructed.

Little did we know on the day of the practice house that yet another Gulf storm was headed our way, this one named Hurricane Rita. The fourth most intense Atlantic hurricane ever recorded, it made landfall on September 24, only a week before our record house would be constructed.

What we initially envisioned for our practice day was to split the crew of more than 1000 workers into two teams. Although we had worked hard to iron out the differences between the trades, we decided that reviving a little healthy competition could go a long way toward improving performance and increasing their interest in the project.

We started to name the two teams Team A and Team B, but we decided against that early on because of what it implied about who the better team was. We went with the more innocuous "Red team" and "Black team."

When we arrived at the field that day, the workers were pumped. Some people joked with me later that the real record set during this event was having that many contractors and laborers show up on time, at the same time, for no pay! For months, their different industries—concrete, trim, paint, etc.— had been experimenting and testing different products and methods. Now it was time to put all of their practice into play.

We fired up the generators as the air horn roared the signal to begin. The time stood at 0:00:00 as both teams took the field like concert-goers rushing the stage of their favorite rock band.

DISASTER FOR ONE TEAM

Soon after the guys on the Black team prepared their lot to receive the concrete, the first of many disasters struck. The concrete dedicated to that team's practice house set up way too quickly. In fact, it happened so fast that much of it set up inside the trucks before they could even pour it out! Five yards set up in the truck (with a yard and a half sitting in the chute), and the rest piled up in a heap behind the truck. The clock read 26:00. Twenty-six minutes and the game was over for that team!

> Five yards set up in the truck (with a yard and a half sitting in the chute), and the rest piled up in a heap behind the truck.

In retrospect, it really wasn't the team's fault entirely. In fact, we learned an important lesson as we dissected everything that contributed to this enormous costly mistake.

It seems obvious now, but one of the larger problems was communication. Eight concrete mixer engines rumbling within several feet of each other make a lot of noise! No one had actually thought of that detail until it was right in front of our faces.

Imagine how difficult it was for those on the concrete crews to hear the time-sensitive communication about what additives to mix when. We had one leader standing between the two practice houses trying to verbally communicate his commands. He was practically screaming the instructions and signals, but still not everyone could hear.

When he saw that the Red house was ready to receive the

concrete, he yelled for them to mix their final additive. However, over the roar of the trucks, the Black team thought he was talking to them, too! Unfortunately, this crew was not at the same point in the process as the Red house.

Thus, when their concrete was ready for them, they were not ready for it.

One of the first things we changed was our communication strategy. We didn't coordinate a series of walkie talkie channels; we went back to basics. We simply devised a flag system to let them know when it was time and what to do. Every eye was on the flag to know when to go.

It sounds so simple, but sometimes the worst problems can be avoided by some simple changes. A red flag meant they would start a certain set of chemicals. A green flag would tell them when to mix the last additive. The leader did not have to yell, because everyone watched for the flag. Problem solved.

PAINFUL RESPONSE

You can imagine the deflated egos of hundreds of disgusted and disgruntled workers who took time off from their paying jobs to spend time at what seemed then like a pointless Saturday morning charade. Without the concrete, there was nowhere to go from there. Dozens of the Black team's other crews of electricians, plumbers, framers and roofers all stood poised, ready to go. But there was nothing for them to do and nothing they could do about it.

> Mistakes in the foundation of any endeavor are costly and can rarely be undone.

For all of our planning, we didn't have a contingency plan for the concrete. Either that sets up or it doesn't. You really can't go anywhere from there. With some things, like a cabinet or a door, you get a chance to come back later and fix it. In the building industry, the foundation is not one of those things.

I've found that to be true of life in general.

Mistakes in the foundation of any endeavor are costly and can rarely be undone. This is why we'll talk more in Chapter Four about the importance of pouring a solid foundation for your work, in your family and in your business and personal relationships. It's that important.

Several of the guys on the Black team threw their hardhats to the ground and walked off the job. Others (who weren't even on that team) observed what had happened and just the *idea* of failure was enough to discourage them. They saw how quickly it was over for the other team and it made them nervous wrecks about their own performance. Such an enormous, public failure spread discouragement like a cancer multiplying through our ranks.

I never saw many of them again. But I wonder now if that wasn't for the best anyway. If they were not able to stick with it and come back from failure, they weren't the right temperament for the job. Success was never a guarantee in this project, although no one ever saw that kind of stalemate coming.

Winston Churchill once said, "Success is the ability to go from one failure after another without any loss of enthusiasm." I'm happy to say that most of the guys who were there on that fateful Saturday did return to the job two weeks later. And they were more excited than ever before. Their subcontractors and supervisors had led some serious cheerleading sessions in the meantime, assuring them it could still work.

It may surprise you to learn that I ended up choosing the two smaller concrete crews from the failed Black team for the actual 2 Hour House project. That meant I had to reject the larger number of concrete crews from the Red team. Imagine how it sounded to the successful team that they were not needed for the real event. We would be using their competition instead. However, this demonstrates an important principle of teamwork we'll discuss later where the decisions that are best for the overall team are usually the best decisions.

ELIMINATING CHAOS

Meanwhile, after the Black team's concrete fiasco, the Red team was still hard at work, but the time dragged as if we were in a slow-motion movie.

When the clock hit 45 minutes, the Red team barely had the framework for the house completed and were sealing the plumbing lines. It was a major accomplishment when crews set the first wall a little after one hour, to resounding cheers from the still hopeful volunteers and spectators present that day. However, everyone knew the game was up when the crane did not lift the roof section until the clock was at 2.5 hours. At four hours, everyone was soaked to the skin, bone-tired and hungry. Yet they were still applying sheetrock, finishing electrical and carpeting some rooms. Later, we began landscaping, unrolling squares of sod and planting trees, which made it look even more like a home.

Although this team also ultimately failed after seven brutal, bloody hours, we learned valuable lessons from our less than stellar practice. The first of which was how to keep everyone following the plan.

> We might as well have tossed the schedule out the window.

WHAT SCHEDULE?

"We might as well have tossed the schedule out the window," I remember telling one of my colleagues in retrospect that day.

It was, in a word, chaos.

Coach Vince Lombardi once remarked, "Practice does not make perfect. Only perfect practice makes perfect." We were a far cry from perfect that day, and simply repeating the techniques we'd practiced for 18 months obviously did not result in perfection. We had to start isolating the problems one by one.

One of the first things that struck me that day was that

everyone on the field looked the same. Plumbers were indistinguishable from roofers; while rockers (sheet rock hangers) blended with the other laborers. No one was able to quickly identify who should be where when, and chaos ensued.

On a very practical note, at the top of my do-list the following Monday was the phone number of a T-shirt company. We ordered colored T-shirts so that on the day of the 2 Hour House, each team had its own distinctly colored shirt. The plumbers wore blue t-shirts. The roofers wore red t-shirts and so on. We even gave the city inspectors black and white referee shirts because they were ready to flag anything we did wrong!

Suddenly, with this one move, we had a visual on all the teams. We even color-coordinated the flow chart so that the schedule indicated who should be on the field (and who should be off) at the correct times.

This simple decision changed the flow of the project instantly and has revolutionized the way I build homes today. All of our job files are color-coordinated with stickers so we know what department that file should be in, from sales to drafting to production. Recognizing a color instead of reading complicated plans or summaries has saved us time and resources. I'm amazed at how the simplest of decisions can make the most impact on the best way to do business. Sometimes we make it all so hard, and it's not necessary.

Also, for the 2 Hour House we established a work zone with cones set 100 feet back from the site so that workers would not be on top of each other. "If you don't have business in the work zone, stay out!" we told everyone. That helped squelch the number of bystanders who were waiting for their job to begin (or

> The simplest decisions can make the most impact on the best way to do business. Sometimes we make it all so hard, and it's not necessary.

had already finished) and were just getting in the way of those trying to do their work!

You've probably experienced that dynamic at work yourself. How about a meeting where only half the participants have any real accountability to the agenda, and the other half acts with disinterest, or worse yet serves as a distraction? Establish your workzone. Make sure those who are in the "workzone" meeting have a responsibility to perform while they're there. Otherwise, they don't really belong in the workzone.

Another dynamic that contributed to the chaotic atmosphere of the practice house was the spider web of airhoses and extension cords that littered the site. Everyone was tripping over the tangled mess of knotted hoses and cords, not to mention growing increasingly frustrated.

For the 2 Hour House, we assigned a leader whose sole responsibility was to tie up the cords and organize them so that they did not get in the way of the work. Again, in retrospect it seemed like such an obvious solution, but only *after* we saw the tangled mass of cords did we make the switch to using as many cordless drills, nailguns and other tools as possible. We should have been doing that all along.

Eliminating chaos and more closely controlling what happened in the workzone created a new culture on the day of the event. We were paying attention this time—to everything and everyone. And they knew it. A rogue red shirt straying away from the task was immediately obvious and correctable. A yellow-shirted tradesperson in the wrong area at the wrong time was easily identified and redirected, much to his relief and ours.

The truth was that we needed more eyes on each piece of the puzzle. For example, at the practice house no one was assigned to tell the electricians when they could go into the roof section and do their thing. They just watched and guessed when it was time to make a move, and more often than not that cascaded into a series of jump-the-gun workmen and a myriad of mistakes.

For the 2 Hour House, Brad stepped in and supervised the entire roof section from A through Z. If an electrician was supposed to go in, he knew exactly when and where he was supposed to go. We had probably assumed too much and focused too little on what we required during the practice house. Eliminating the assumptions helped everyone feel more confident in their role and perform better.

Have you found that people function best within clearly defined boundaries? It's true in family dynamics. Children may say they don't like boundaries or being told what to do, but studies have shown what any good parent already knows: kids are less stressed and function better when they know what is expected of them and are held accountable to healthy rules of family living. On the site of the 2 Hour House, there was no question that workers' performance improved as we raised what was expected of them in what was now a much more controlled environment.

> Workers' performance improved as we raised what was expected of them.

LOWEST POINT

In hindsight, we were entirely too self-assured going in to our practice day. To prove my point, we had not even brought any extra water or made a fallback plan for lunch. Lunch? We thought we'd all be eating at home by noon, celebrating our victory and recounting great stories about how well the morning's competition had gone.

Instead, by one or two that afternoon, everyone was starving, performance was at a standstill and attitudes were really souring. To make matters worse, the type of brick siding we tried that morning was also a dismal failure, causing a frantic new product search in the weeks following. We didn't even try to finish it out because it was so complicated for our tradespeople to use.

After seven grueling hours of continuously getting off track and back on again, I stopped the clock and told everyone to go home. I was the last one to leave that day, and it was a very lonely moment.

Inside, I was completely crushed, but I could not afford to let anyone else (not even my friends Brad and Carey) see my disappointment.

All of the criticisms that had been hurled our way over the past 18 months now whispered in my ear with sinister conviction. For the first time since I began this challenge, I was sincerely down about the entire project.

But it was too late to pull the plug and not go through with it. We had a phenomenal marketing team who had promoted this event all over the East Texas area and beyond. Television reporters and camera crews from all over the nation were scheduled to arrive (although the hurricanes definitely affected the planned coverage). I had already completed several local interviews and articles about the upcoming event.

> Several people encouraged me to face facts. It wasn't going to happen. I should just give up right now.

Billboards advertising the 2 Hour House throughout the community were already in place. The irony of it all hit hard as I drove home later that evening and passed one of them. "2 Hour House. Come See Us Set a World Record."

With images of the dismal failure I'd just witnessed and only 14 days to salvage it, the words seemed almost like a joke. I remembered telling the TABA members my idea 18 months ago. Half of them were immediately excited and half of them said I was completely crazy, although all of them supported me.

"Maybe we *are* crazy," I remember thinking to myself as I made my way around the city loop toward home. In fact, several people came up to me that weekend, took me aside and encouraged me to face facts. It wasn't going to happen. I should just give up right now before I wasted any more time and money or embarrassed myself and hundreds of others with me.

That afternoon, it occurred to me with sudden clarity that there were *reasons* why no one had set a new world record in over twenty years. It was tough. It was enormously complicated. It seemed like too much. I knew it would require significant courage to come back from the two back-to-back defeats we'd experienced that day. Not just one practice house had failed, but two. And I wasn't sure that I had it in me to take one more step.

At that moment, it felt as though we were closer to going up in flames rather than going down in history. It was almost as if this incredible failure somehow tapped into alternating layers of doubt and strength deep inside of me that I didn't even know were there. I'd been a pretty successful guy up to that point. I had never experienced the depth of human failure like I had that weekend.

BORN ENTREPRENEUR

I knew I was born to be an entrepreneur from the time I was in elementary school. While all my other friends were into video games and soccer tournaments, I was always cooking up a new business.

I remember one time I bought 100 watches from my neighbor for around 100 dollars. The next day at school, my mom made sure that I brought my books, lunch and school supplies, and I made sure I brought my inventory of watches. On the playground that day, I began selling the watches to my friends for five dollars each. They thought it was a bargain, but the principal thought otherwise. But that was just the beginning.

When it came time every year for students to participate in school fundraising (selling already overpriced candy bars to your relatives and neighbors), I decided to take a different approach. It was Christmastime, and I stuffed my assigned number of chocolate Santa boxes into my backpack and went to work on my business plan. I took out a pen and wrote down some numbers. I figured if I could make a couple of dollars off of each chocolate Santa sale, then the school would earn its money and I would realize a profit, too. When I got home that day, I carefully scratched off all the prices from each Santa and proceeded to mark them up a couple of dollars each.

I figured if I was going to walk around the neighborhood dragging around this chocolate inventory, I ought to at least be compensated for my time. At the end of the month, my teachers were so proud. I turned in all the money I was supposed to raise for school. Much to my dad's chagrin, I had turned Santa into my own cash cow. I was in fifth grade learning about history and math, but my most valuable lessons came from what I was learning about how to turn a profit!

> I was in fifth grade learning about history and math, but my most valuable lessons came from what I was learning about how to turn a profit!

Around that time I also started my own lawn-mowing company. I began when I was 10 years old, using a push mower to mow several yards in the neighborhood. I still remember when I'd saved enough money to invest in a riding lawnmower. I thought I was really something then!

By the time I was a young teen, I had three "employees." Even though I was several years their junior—I didn't even drive yet—we started making money hand over fist, so they didn't seem to mind giving their "boss" a ride to work. Word spread and I soon had a well-established lawn business, complete with landscaping services.

I got my hardship license at 15, bought a car with more of my savings and drove myself to all my sites, business cards in hand and lawnmowers in tow. I was still only a teenager with a curfew, but I was earning two or three thousand dollars a month during the high season. I worked and saved every penny I had.

My dad was a home builder and people figured I would eventually go into the family business as a young adult. However, my need for speed led me elsewhere. I was an amateur racecar driver from the time I was out of high school and into my twenties, racing two nights a week at the dirt tracks for four years. I drove for myself for two years, learning the ropes and supporting my "career" with the money I'd made from my winnings, sponsors and my lawn business.

However, doing it this way was very expensive and I told myself my career would hit the end of the road unless I began driving for someone else. When I drove someone else's car, the job became so much easier. All I had to do was show up and drive around the track. I kept 25% of every win, and I won far more often than I lost. I was married to a wonderful woman, and we were soon expecting our first child. Everything up to that point had seemed to come easy for me.

However, fast forward several years to the weekend of September, 2005. I came to a point where things weren't so easy. And I wasn't sure what I would do.

> I came to a point where things weren't so easy. And I wasn't sure what I would do.

STARTING AGAIN

"It ain't over 'til it's over!" That was Yogi Berra's famous answer to a reporter when he was managing the New York Mets in July 1973, the year I was born. The Mets were about nine games out of first place at the time of that interview. However, they went on to win the division.

The weekend of the practice house, I had that nine-games-out kind of feeling. However, even though our practice was far from perfect, I believe our failure served to teach us volumes. Our practice wasn't perfect; but somehow it perfected us. It strengthened our resolve. It made us appreciate teamwork. It made us hungry for victory.

Monday morning, I called my Executive Board members Brad and Carey and said what they least expected to hear. I even half-surprised myself when I heard my own voice.

"Man, we've got this thing licked. When can we get together?"

My call could not have come at a better (or worse) time. My friends and colleagues Brad and Carey both were as down as they'd ever been. After Saturday's fiasco, it seemed like this project that had consumed them and taken them away from their families and true vocations for the past six months had just been worthless.

Brad recalls thinking that his father's ominous prediction had almost come true that weekend. In light of the disaster Saturday, it looked like someone *was* going to get killed on this project and Brad wasn't so sure he wouldn't be the first one to go!

"I was ready to throw in the towel," Brad concedes. "I was overwhelmed."

Even though I experienced the same level of frustration and doubt as Carey and Brad after that day, I knew I had a responsibility to tough it out and keep everyone going.

And so I did.

History is replete with the names of those who tried and failed. But we know their names only if they tried again until they succeeded. Anyone who has done or will do anything noteworthy has more than one failure in his or her past. However, history does not record the names of those who tried, failed and never tried again. Those guys go off into anonymity and we never hear of them anymore.

I didn't want to lump my name with the rest of them; I wanted to be alongside the likes of a Macy, a Creasey or a Ruth.

R. H. Macy failed to make a go of his department store idea seven times before he succeeded in New York. John Creasey, an English novelist, was rejected over 700 times before he published the first of what would be several hundred books. Babe Ruth had to strike out 1330 times in order to also hit 714 home runs. I believed that the only real failure that could come out of this was the failure to try again.

On Tuesday, with my friends Brad and Carey at my side, we resumed the meetings—with all the members of the Quality

Council and their various team leaders present.

Like a football team on the morning after the big game, we watched clips we'd videoed from the practice house event and discussed the highlights of what we did wrong and what we did well. We made a crucial decision to combine the houses and just do one 2 Hour House instead of trying to make it a competition. We would have one combined team trying to beat the clock, not each other.

I made sure that we focused our sights on what was ahead and drove the momentum and enthusiasm toward it full steam. And yet, there was no denying we'd all been deeply rattled by the practice house experience. It was too soon to tell if we'd adjusted the plan in all the ways we needed to. We wouldn't know until that fateful morning if all our practice would make perfect or make for another perfect disaster.

> We would have one combined team trying to beat the clock, not each other.

To Think About

- Do you think practice really does make perfect? Why or why not?

- Why can failure sometimes teach you more than success?

- When was a time you learned this type of lesson?

- Winston Churchill said, "Success is the ability to go from one failure after another without any loss of enthusiasm." Why is enthusiasm so important to reaching your goals?

- What kinds of people and situations hamper your enthusiasm? What can you do to overcome them?

- Do you have the right players on your team?

NOTES

This was the opportunity to be a part of something so much bigger than what I would normally take on by myself. The greatest lesson I learned was the importance of a firm foundation. Take the time to get your foundation right, and everything else will come together so much easier.

Kevin G. Koop
Chairman
Countertop Committee

NEVER NEGLECT THE FUNDAMENTALS

Identify the fundamentals and build everything else on them

When the first headlights appeared over the ridge of the subdivision the morning of the 2 Hour House, my pulse began to race. What is called a "Blue Norther" in Texas had blown through the night before, bringing the temperature down 20 degrees, again atypical for that time of year and definitely different from the sauna-like heat two weeks prior.

For the day of the event, we had rented a grandstand to hold several thousand spectators who had come out to watch. Families, leaders in the community, representatives from the charities we were supporting, media personnel and others in the building industry also made their way to the field to watch the event unfold.

To make an even bigger statement, our marketing team had planned an opening ceremony, with the National Anthem and a skydiving exhibition. After the last sky diver touched down, the crowd erupted into cheers and we sounded the horn to begin the construction.

The time was 00:00:00.

Teams of men and women sprung into action like wooden

toys suddenly come to life. The adrenaline was flowing and activity was everywhere. In its first few moments of life, I could see that this project was already nothing like its predecessor, the practice house.

For one thing, each team's movement—a band of green shirts here; a swatch of red there—was coordinated and synchronized.

WORKERS SPRING INTO ACTION AS WE SOUND THE HORN TO BEGIN CONSTRUCTION.

Barrel-chested tradesmen in steel-toed boots and hardhats moved with the grace of stage actors, moving from point to point on the field.

It was electric.

I looked over at my friend Carey and grinned. He was lit up like a Christmas tree with a walkie talkie in each hand, an earpiece in one ear, a cellphone strapped to his waist and a megaphone tucked under his arm. Everything was a go. First up, the concrete.

DO THE FUNDAMENTALS

The stories behind the concrete remind me of the importance of identifying and mastering the fundamentals in whatever you do. Innovation and spin-off services are great, but the fundamentals of what you do best always comprise the concrete or foundation of your business. It may be sales. It may be marketing. It may be product development. It's impossible to say that one of these is more important than the other. All fundamentals—including your mission statement, vision statement and values—are important because they work together to form the foundation.

Think about it this way: What is the foundation of an airplane? The airframe? The engines? The avionics? Each is fundamental to an airplane; and together, they comprise the whole plane. You can't say one part is more important than the other because they work in tandem.

Any relationship you have in your life today relies on all of the fundamentals of friendship (such as trust and honesty) working together. If any one of those fundamentals is missing or damaged in some way, the relationship suffers, so don't take any of them for granted.

The foundation determines what kind of "house" (a business or a relationship) you want to build.

Raising a family works in much the same way. Establishing healthy boundaries and rules in a young child's life is crucial because of how it affects them later in life as the child grows and matures. A family in emotional and relational chaos is a family who never took the necessary time early on to establish family guidelines and expectations.

However, it can also relate to any undertaking where practicing the fundamentals and having a good foundation is critical to future success. Putting the fundamentals in place applies to business executives, teachers, students, athletes—anyone facing any new challenge, task, relationship or endeavor. The foundation determines what kind of "house" (a business or a relationship) you want to build. Everyone has a different house—it may be a single story or a multi-story house; it may be a traditional or a ranch style house. However, the foundation is what always determines the height and shape of the house. How you start is directly related to how you finish. I tell my teams all the time: "Never neglect the fundamentals." Why? Because you will build everything related to your goal on them.

CONCRETE DETAILS

The first team to react to the drastic change in the weather was the concrete. All summer into the early fall they had perfected a mix based on 80-90 degree weather. In the twelve-hour period preceding the event, the temperature plummeted, sending this team back to the drawing board.

Early that morning, they were hard at work back at the concrete plant readjusting the formula and hoping they would either get it right or just get lucky. Anything less than perfection would spoil the entire endeavor—we knew that too well.

There was never any doubt that the concrete was one of the most important aspects of the 2 Hour House project. Sure, we could have built the house on pier and beam, solving many issues from the beginning and even reducing our time.

MULTIPLE CREWS BEGIN DIGGING TRENCHES FOR PLUMBING.

But we would not have set the record we had in mind.

The expectation was for a solid concrete slab house. We had to go head to head with our greatest challenges in order to accomplish our goal.

The foundation began with laying form boards on the dirt.

Then the workers outlined the footprint of the home in two by sixes as another crew began digging the necessary trenches for plumbing. They dug together in rhythm, not unlike a university crew team on the waters of the Hudson River. Men on either side of the trench swung alternating shovels full of dirt, moving so fast in a blur of perfect unison.

The concrete was mixed at the plant with its initial chemicals, waiting to add the final dosage until they arrived on site, 25 minutes away from the plant. Saving precious minutes, I had arranged for a police escort for the trucks from the plant to the site. The scene was surreal—eight gleaming white concrete mixers surrounded by several motorcycle police, sirens blaring, cutting through the early morning traffic on the Tyler loop.

When the big trucks arrived, the crowd cheered as spotters moved them into position. The chutes were poised above every section of the floorplan, ready to dump concrete at the appointed time. Twenty-eight seconds later, 48 cubic yards of poured out into the forms. And this time, we were ready.

LESSONS LEARNED

Here are some time-tested principles that I learned about giving the foundation of your goal the attention it deserves.

- The foundation says a lot about who you are—as a person, as a company, as a family, etc.
- Communicate the importance of your foundation to others.
- Test your foundational values in real life situations.
- Don't rest on your foundation...build on it!

PRINCIPLE ONE
The foundation says a lot about who you are.

Your fundamentals determine a lot about you. It doesn't take long for someone to figure out what you most value. Values are those things that have intrinsic worth to us. They are qualities that we hold dear and strive to live. If you want to know what you or your company really values, ask someone. Ask several different people. (Preferably someone who does not work for or with you!) You may be surprised by the answers.

You see, unfortunately for many companies, families and individuals, there is a disconnect between what we say we value and the way we prioritize our commitments. Ralph Waldo Emerson, whose writings made great observations about human behavior, once noted, "Who you are speaks so loudly I can't hear what you are saying." Your values may be buried beneath company policies and procedures. Or maybe they're hidden by a smokescreen of complicated jargon, logos, etc.

> It doesn't take long for someone to figure out what you most value.

In our case, the foundation we chose to use said a lot about who we are. We were not interested in compromising by going the pier-and-beam route or working off of a pre-poured slab. If we were going to build a record, we were going to do it right and challenge ourselves to the hilt to come up with a way that it could be done.

It also said a lot about our commitment to integrity and our values when we decided to meet or exceed code throughout the home, including a 10-year structural warranty.

For example, we used a newly developed termite protection method that is better than traditional spray methods but would only take two minutes to perform. Instead of spraying the foundation for termite protection, we used a termite barrier—a stainless steel screen that wrapped around the sewer plumbing in the foundation. It formed a barrier between potential termites and the pipes. Additionally, the formula for the concrete we used was quick, but it was not a compromise in quality. We actually more than tripled the standard pounds-per-square-inch rating that is acceptable in any modern home because we wanted to ensure it would stand the test of time.

There are so many benefits to thinking consciously and deliberately about the fundamental values that make up your company or your family or your personal life. As it relates to the 2 Hour House, I can say that when you know and commit to your values, decision-making becomes a lot easier.

I am proud to say that we put the home up for sale soon after its construction and it sold very quickly—actually the day after it was on the market. As of this writing, nearly a year later, we have received no complaints from the owner. I believe that is due in part to the quality construction we invested into the home.

Today, the home is indistinguishable from the other quality homes in the subdivision. Only a plaque remains outside the front door identifying it as the record-setting 2 Hour House. Of the thousands and thousands of decisions that were made in the process of planning and building this home, sticking to our values made each one easier. Eliminating options that would save time but undermine the quality was a no-brainer. Our commitment drove us to consider only the best alternatives.

> We actually more than tripled the standard pounds-per-square-inch rating that is acceptable in any modern home.

Principle Two
Communicate the importance of your foundation to others.

We communicated our commitment to making the foundation the best it could be in several ways. First, we spent the most time on it. Dick and his team of researchers began the process of research nearly one year in advance. They ran test after test trying to determine which product would function to scale in the lab and in real life as well.

Second, on the day of the project, we left no doubt in anyone's mind about the importance of this piece of the puzzle when eight concrete trucks arrived amid a full police escort, lights flashing and horns honking.

Now, that was some important concrete.

Are you doing anything in your business to demonstrate your commitment to your values in unmistakable ways? Is it immediately obvious to others that the customer is vital to the success of your company?

Consider your personal life. Do you organize your life's priorities in such a way that you demonstrate to observers what you are about? Could someone read your checkbook and determine your commitments right away? How about what your daily calendar or palm pilot says about your values?

One engineer for the concrete company who had come out to watch the event that day (but had not been in the practice

CONCRETE TRUCKS ARRIVE ON THE SCENE, LIGHTS FLASHING AND HORNS HONKING!

meetings) saw how the chemicals were being staged and grew alarmed at the unconventional methods. He reprimanded the workers for not doing it right—he'd never seen it done that way—and actually tried to interfere and stop them. Other workers saw what was going on and tried to convince him to let them do it.

But he would not be deterred. Finally, a supervisor took him by the arm to physically remove him from the area before he ruined the entire batch!

Those guys were sold. They were sold out to the unusual way the concrete had to be formulated in order to succeed. So much so that they were willing to risk with ruthless abandon crossing anyone, even an intelligent engineer, who represented the status quo.

Are the people in your organization so sold out to your values and the way your company does its thing that when they see a potential threat to their corporate value system, they immediately take it off the field?

> Have you empowered the lowest person in your chain of command with a sense of loyalty to the mission?

Have you empowered the lowest person in your chain of command with this sense of loyalty to the mission?

All of the people on Dick's crew were wildly committed to their part in the project because they realized the importance of what they were doing. The weight of the entire project figuratively and literally rested on their shoulders. "The guys knew the success of the project was up to them in the beginning. I told them it could all be over with in fifteen minutes if they didn't do this part right. And they didn't want to be the ones to let the others down. No one on the team wanted to be the one who dropped the ball," recalled Dick.

PRINCIPLE THREE
Test your fundamental values in real life situations.

In the lab, the concrete set up perfectly. In fact, they could manufacture conditions so perfect that concrete would set up in a matter of minutes. But remember, the day of the 2 Hour House, the temperature had dropped significantly, requiring a last minute run back to the lab to adjust the concrete formula to account for this change.

Fortunately, the formulators had already anticipated the

possibility of foul weather (they say in East Texas if you don't like the weather, just wait a minute). So, they built in a way to accommodate this variance in the basic formula. And they could do it on the fly.

Although they discovered the specific properties that would make for a quick-drying, self-leveling concrete in the lab, they did not limit their tests to lab practice alone. In the lab, they used very small doses in perfect conditions. There came a time (several in fact) that they had to test it in real life using doses that were large enough to scale to simulate a slab for a house. In fact, according to Dick, the engineering department in Cleveland who discovered the correct formula said, "In the lab, it will do such and such. But you're going to have to get out there and mix this stuff up to see if it really works."

If customers catch on to your mission statement because of how you run your business, then it is worth something.

Undoubtedly, you have observed organizations that have spent way too much time in the "lab" and not enough time in the real world. They may schedule meeting after meeting and corporate retreats to discuss, fine-tune and rehash their mission statement, vision statement and values without practical application.

The problem with this strategy is that a mission statement that has nothing to do with business in the real world is basically worthless. If customers catch on to your mission statement because of how you run your business, then it is worth something. Do your customers know your mission statement?

I've known companies, and you have too, whose executives spent so much time and resources on nailing a fine-sounding mission statement that they have lost interest in and enthusiasm for applying them in real life. You can focus on the values so much that you never take them out for a spin and show the world what you are about.

I'll never forget a story Dick shared about some of the workers who were present during the testing phase of the concrete. These were tough concrete contractors who had worked around concrete all their lives and simply did not believe concrete could set up in minutes instead of hours. Dick's crews, who had been working with the experiments all summer, warned those standing in the forms waiting for it to pour that they would have about five minutes to work with it and then they would have to move out because it would begin its initial set.

However, on that particular afternoon, the visitors got carried away in conversation in the middle of their work as the load was being poured. Thinking they had all the time in the world, they continued standing around talking to each other in the middle of the test pad. Suddenly the mixture hardened up on them, rendering them immobile and embarrassed! Dick's crew actually had to help them out of the concrete, leaving their boots right where they had been standing!

You can be sure that those guys became believers that day.

What are you doing in your company to make believers out of the skeptics who say it can't really work in real life? What are you doing to show them in undeniable ways that your business services work in real life?

What are you doing to make the words of your mission statement jump right off the page for your employees and customers?

I believe this illustrates a principle for other key relationships, too. Are your expectations for your family based on reality? Sometimes we want to have the perfect family with perfect children who never do anything to upset that vision we've had of what raising a family would be like. Life in the lab is safe; but real life, despite its constant challenges, is far better.

As the father of four girls, I've noticed that in real life, children struggle with authority from the time you first begin to teach them the word, "no" to the time they become tenuous adolescents and grow up into young adulthood.

Maybe it's time to revisit the fundamentals of your

relationship with your kids and see if your expectations for them and the way your family should operate have left room for real life to happen. As John Lennon once said, "Life is what happens when you are busy making other plans."

The same might be said of the way you interact with your colleagues and/or staff. Sometimes our expectations for ourselves and for those with whom we work are so high that they are not even realistic. People make mistakes, and real life management recognizes that inevitability. If you are in management, coaching others to where you want them to be takes time and patience. In the same way, it takes time to

CREWS POURED THE ENTIRE SLAB IN **28** SECONDS.

meld together as a team of colleagues—a team that has wrestled with failure has the potential to go on to great success because it has brought them closer together. We all probably prefer a perfect world to the one we're living in…but don't miss out on what is real in your relationships.

PRINCIPLE FOUR
Don't rest on your foundation…build on it!

As important as the foundation of your endeavor is, don't be content with it. Imagine if someone contracted with me to build them a home, and I worked the next six months without a single site visit by the owner.

On the appointed day that they expect to sign the papers, imagine their surprise if on their beautiful, hand-picked lot, all there was to see was a gleaming new mailbox in front of a grey slab? Not a single two-by-four, shingle, window or door in sight.

"Where is our house?" they would ask bewildered. I could give them my best spiel on how we had spared no expense in providing them with a flawless foundation that would be sure to hold up for several generations of their family.

> Work the fundamentals and build a strong foundation. But don't stop there. Build!

However, you know they would not be happy homeowners. Foundations are important, but remember their sole purpose is to support all of your subsequent endeavors.

Spend a lot of time on the fundamentals of your relationships with others. Do your due diligence on the values and mission statement of your company. Work the fundamentals and build a strong foundation. But don't stop there. Build!

READY TO POUR

Once on site, the concrete workers feverishly dosed the batches with the final chemical mix. For every truck, there were six people working to perform the required tasks. Every driver had a back-up driver in the cab with him just in case. There were three people and one supervisor who formed an assembly line to pass the chemicals and dose the mix. One handed the chemicals up to the mid-way point; one accepted the dose at the mid-way point and passed it to the third crew member who actually put it inside the drum. Of course, on a typical job, there is one driver who does it all—and not under the watchful eye of thousands of others.

Amazingly, they poured 48 cubic yards of self-leveling

concrete in 28 seconds as the finishers began fervently raking and spreading the dark grey mixture into the corners and sides of the grid.

As promised, the concrete began to set within 12 minutes, hardening from the middle outward. What would normally take place hours after pouring concrete (to ensure it was dry enough) happened in seven minutes when men walked onto the concrete to snap chalk lines marking the placement of the walls.

After about 20 minutes the concrete was strong enough to drive a car on, but we wanted to wait a few more minutes for it to set up just as an extra precaution. Meanwhile, the concrete crews were busy dosing their trucks with chemicals to protect the trucks from the leftover concrete inside the drums that was sure to harden!

SEE IT TO BELIEVE IT

The hundreds of workers and contractors on site could not believe their eyes. Several found themselves inexplicably drawn to place their hands on it as if to disprove what their eyes were seeing. Although I had been to many of their test practices throughout the summer, even I got caught up in the moment! I pressed my own hand onto

PRESSING MY OWN HAND ONTO THE SLAB—EVEN I WAS AMAZED.

a drying section, shaking my head in awe!

A typical home's slab is rated at 3000 psi, but because we were committed to meeting and exceeding code on the 2 Hour House, the concrete we used was rated over 10,000 psi, which set the inspectors' minds at ease.

After about 20 minutes, the concrete was entirely set and ready to build upon. That's when things really got cooking and the most amazing undertaking by our builders' association began to unfold with a rapid pace.

To Think About

- What are your fundamental values? By answering the following questions, you can help clarify what is most important to you: What story inspired you or made a major impression on you? What event or occurrence moved you to make changes in your life? What is the secret to life that you would pass on to future generations?

- What are you doing in your company to make believers out of the skeptics?

- Are you satisfied with the progress you're making as you build on the foundation of your family, business or personal life goals? Why or why not?

NOTES

You could say each of us had a crash course in Home Building 101. My job was the plumbing, and even though it was a large part of the whole project, it was no more important than the smallest task to complete the home in record time. As one of the more "seasoned" builders involved, I learned with the right people you can do anything! And we did.

Tom Utz
Chairman
Plumbing Committee

DETAILS, DETAILS, DETAILS

See the big picture and motivate others to fulfill the smallest detail

As the concrete hardened, the walls were clearly marked and assembled in sections scattered over the field and manned by pairs of workers. We installed the electrical components into the walls before they were hand-carried and seamed together section by section. The exterior sections came together as continuous walls that ran the length of the house. Teams of workers picked up and delivered each exterior wall and placed it into position, with one person per stud carrying the wall and setting it into place.

At this point, the adrenaline was running a little high and people got carried away with enthusiasm. Several walls were picked up in the incorrect sequence and we lost valuable minutes sorting through which walls were supposed to go where. For the first and only time that day, we had to get out the plans and recheck the placement.

It's important to remember that half of the people who ended up working on the event day had never been able to practice their responsibilities because one practice house had never gotten off the ground. That cut the amount of those who had practiced in half. And those whose responsibilities fell after the seven hour cut-off time for the other practice house did not get to practice either! For several hundred people on the day of the event, the record-setting house was *their* first-time practice house.

If we could do it again, we would save several minutes in this one area alone because everyone would have been able to rehearse at least once. However, we eventually did place the walls in the right order and continued on.

We began implementing our inside-out strategy to hang drywall and insulation. As I explained, typically the exterior of the walls are completed first and then the interior is stuffed with insulation and the process of hanging drywall begins. However, if we did the exterior walls first as we normally would, we would essentially seal off all of our entry points into the home for sheets of drywall and other materials to be brought in, leaving only the front and back doors for entry and exit.

> You have to *know* what it takes before you can say you "have" what it takes to get a tough job done.

Hundreds of people were continuously filing in and out of those entry ways, so once again we purposefully turned the traditional building method on its ear and brought our materials in through the walls. This allowed multiple points of entry through the studs where laborers could hand materials to the "rockers" (the workers hanging the sheetrock or drywall) who could be hanging it in place.

As we worked our way from the middle outward, we were able to haul out trash and scraps the same way we'd brought in the materials. Once all of the drywall sheets were hung inside and the insulation material was installed, we began to seal the exterior walls with plywood, siding and paint. Although we had set aside ten minutes to paint the interior of the home, we cut that time in half and almost in half again—painting the entire home in about three minutes! Unfortunately, we don't have this unbelievable achievement documented on video because once the paint guns fired up, the camera guys were out of there!

Thousands and thousands of tiny details began coming into place as the walls, roof and interior began to take shape. The goal for the 2 Hour House was to build upon a solid foundation. Once we began putting up the walls, it began to look like a real house.

Do you know the details of your endeavor? You have to *know* what it takes before you can say you "have" what it takes to get a tough job done. Are your people motivated to fulfill the goal down to the smallest detail?

That's what it means to see the big picture, but also motivate others to fulfill even the smallest, seemingly

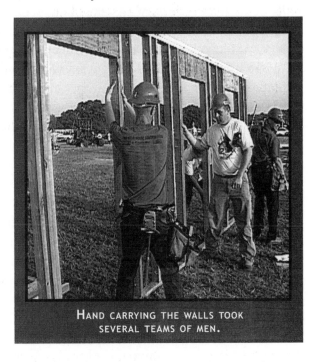

HAND CARRYING THE WALLS TOOK SEVERAL TEAMS OF MEN.

insignificant detail. This part of the story illustrates the importance of mastering the details of your goal.

MASTERING DETAILS ELIMINATES ASSUMPTIONS

In my three-ring notebooks, we had accounted for every detail down to the last doorstop and electrical plate. Documenting goes a long way toward eliminating assumptions. When people ask me for a tip about managing the details, I often tell them, "Write it down!" Writing and documenting details does several things for the good of your endeavor.

For one, it builds consistency in your system and means nothing is taken for granted. Let's face it—people grow complacent. Details get overlooked. Assuming people will "get" what it takes to do something right is something a leader does to his or her own peril.

One assumption that took place on the day of the 2 Hour House resulted in the only mistake the concrete crews made that day. Because of the unusual mix of chemicals, everything had to be done a certain way even long after the trucks had backed away from the site. One of the guys was washing his truck out the incorrect way, and it turns out that he was the only one who was not at the practice house weeks earlier. A veteran concrete driver, he assumed he knew the correct way to wash his truck out—something he'd done hundreds of times before. But this time was different, and the way he did it could have ruined the machinery.

> **Mastering details allows you to improve your product at all times and in several ways.**

Details keep people open to learning. It removes some of the mystery of what it takes to be successful because they learn to master the details with consistency. Success naturally follows. Mastering details allows you a way to improve your product at all times and in several ways. Sometimes the smallest tweak to a detail can make all the difference.

In this instance, we had catalogued every electrical outlet in the walls. They were labeled and color-coordinated because several crews of electricians would be installing them throughout the house at the same time. We thought we had our bases covered, but we soon discovered (thankfully before the 2 Hour House) that one more level of details needed to be covered for this step.

You see, every electrician installed the outlets to the same code, but each company had its own standards for the *way* they installed them into the walls. Some crews used their hammer and measured from the bottom of the hammer to the head to mark the placement of a wall outlet. Some put the hammer on an electrical cover plate and measured from there.

If the outlet placement for the 2 Hour House had not been standardized, outlets would have been scattered all over the place like piano notes on sheet music!

This said a great deal to me about eliminating assumptions. One would think that knowing exactly what wall to install it on, when to install it and how many wall outlets were needed in a room would be enough information to cover the job.

Not so if you have four different crews operating with different standards for placement. Eliminating assumptions means everyone is using the same playbook to execute the plays. It may mean that you as the leader make sure your managers cover more information than you think anyone needs to know. In fact, we standardized every detail in the completion of the house to unify all the crews we had working on site.

> **Assumptions are tricky things that trip up everyone once in a while. I'm just glad we caught ours before it was too late.**

When someone came on board to the 2 Hour House project, we followed a simple procedure with them: Enlist, Empower and Encourage. We enlisted them to a specific area or trade. They knew what team they were on and who their supervisors were.

We empowered them with tasks that assumed nothing, but entrusted them with everything. In other words, we gave them a monumental task, but we talked them through every step of the process so that they did not question what was expected.

Finally, we encouraged them along the way. This is the tone a good leader takes when eliminating assumptions. It's not talking down to the individuals as if they do not know their trade. It means making them feel like they are part of something so important and significant that their smallest contribution to it will be their greatest success.

Assumptions are tricky things that trip up everyone once in a while. I'm just glad we caught ours before it was too late.

MASTERING DETAILS INCREASES SPEED WITHOUT SACRIFICING QUALITY

We were always looking for ways to shave off minutes and even seconds from our time. Therefore, we employed value engineering, which simply means designing with minimal waste and maximum efficiency in mind for this 3 bedroom, 2 bath, 2 car garage home. For example, we designed the floorplan so that the plumbing ran down a central path in the home from the kitchen to the laundry area to the bathrooms. This one detail alone was a key timesaver for us.

Increasing the speed at which you can execute details like this without sacrificing quality generally means more business. That is, if you're consistent. Sure, you could do a one-time rush

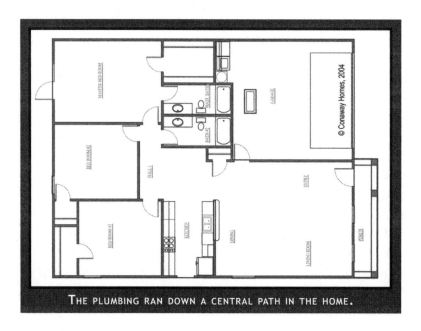

THE PLUMBING RAN DOWN A CENTRAL PATH IN THE HOME.

job for an important customer and focus all your attention on it. But that's not what I'm talking about. I'm talking about doing it faster and better on a consistent basis—and doing that so well that it becomes business as usual.

Take express mail delivery throughout the world as an example. In the days before this kind of service, shippers had no effective way to accommodate time-sensitive shipments such as medicines, computer parts and electronics. In the mid-sixties, airfreight routes were slow, not efficiently planned and had no guarantee for delivery by a certain date. It was extremely difficult to get packages and other airfreight delivered in a timely manner, unless you were willing to pay exorbitant fees or were willing to risk that your package might or might not arrive on time.

That's when the idea for express mail began to take shape. The goal was to develop speedy package delivery within one to two days, anywhere in the world—all without sacrificing quality. Today, there are multiple express mail companies with a fleet of aircraft and other carriers that deliver packages around the globe twenty-four hours a day. Their couriers log millions of miles a day because they have developed a way to increase productivity and efficiency without risking the quality people demand when delivering their most important packages.

> Increasing how fast you can serve your customers and meet their needs doesn't mean taking shortcuts. It just means thinking about the outcome a different way.

There is a myth in business today that says quality takes time. While that may be true with things like aging a fine wine or creating a masterpiece, it is generally not true in business. In fact, it is more often the opposite.

Increasing how fast you can serve your customers and meet

their needs doesn't mean taking shortcuts. It just means thinking about the outcome a different way. This was the principle behind the 2 Hour House.

Understandably, many people who first heard about our project were concerned about the quality of its construction. Or, if they knew anything about the construction industry at all, they would assume it was a pier-and-beam instead of a concrete slab foundation. Some even wondered if we didn't assemble some of the pieces earlier in the week or pour the foundation days before. Frankly, some people asked me sarcastically, "Did it fall apart after you were finished?"

Here's the irony. Because each piece of material in this house had to be perfect, we made sure that it was exactly that: perfect. For example, we personally picked each piece of lumber that went into this house, ensuring that each stud would be perfectly straight. We upgraded our countertops to use granite tile in the kitchen. We even lined the closets with a high-end material that gave the homeowners an unexpected upgrade, but at the same time it allowed us to avoid slowing down to tape and bed drywall inside such a small space.

Some thought we would have to overlook attention to detail in order to meet our goals. However, it was actually just the opposite. Our attention to detail enabled us to meet and even exceed our goals. If we did not have perfect, quality lumber, every other detail would not have fallen into place like it should.

The myth in many businesses is that quality naturally suffers in proportion to an increase in speed and efficiency. We were quick, but we weren't about quick fixes! Having the housing inspectors on sight to scrutinize and inspect each part of the process held us accountable to meet or beat code at every turn. In addition to Renee, the chief building inspector, the city supplied International Code Council certified inspectors, including a master electrician, master plumber and a master framing and foundation representative.

Some of the new products and techniques developed for the 2 Hour House were so good that others utilized them beyond the project as well. Because of their unique properties, they were often too expensive to make their way into everyday building practices, but some of the products had other uses. For example, the Texas Department of Transportation heard about the fast-drying cement that Dick had developed. Dick was able to modify the formula so that TXDOT could begin using it to repair highways.

Instead of shutting down an entire highway overnight to repair a pothole, they could use this quick-drying cement and have the highway up and running again in a matter of hours. "They could tear up a highway at six in the evening and have traffic back on it at nine that same night," Dick said of this new initiative. It solved their problems quickly and efficiently with a minimum amount of safety concerns since they did not have to block off traffic on the interstate for more than a few hours. Just another example of how speed and quality can go together without canceling each other out.

I am confident that other builders could use the system we developed for the 2 Hour House, in terms of scheduling and organization, as a template for replicating other houses. If you were to stretch it out for one week instead of a couple of hours, I believe it would be possible to build one home per week for fifty-two weeks a year. And build the perfect house each time.

MASTERING DETAILS MEANS LEARNING THE COMPRESSOR CONCEPT

Another lesson has to do with not taking your eye off the big picture when you're watching the details. The practice house showed us how neglecting several important details contributed to the breakdown of the big picture. I've already shared some of the details we overlooked during the practice house.

This one, however, was a biggie.

I fondly remember it as learning the Compressor Concept. Let me explain.

That year, we weren't the only ones to set a record. Katrina was the sixth-strongest Atlantic hurricane ever recorded and the third-strongest landfalling U.S. hurricane on record. The storm of the century formed in late August and dashed many of our original plans for renting the necessary equipment. Understandably, with most of the north-central Gulf Coast in ruins, FEMA had dibs on every piece of power equipment for hundreds and thousands of miles. Suddenly, both of the generators we'd reserved for the practice houses, along with two cranes big enough to hoist a 30,000 pound roof, became scarce as diamonds. This crisis arose about five weeks before our scheduled date for the 2 Hour House and just before our practice house.

> Suddenly, both of the generators and cranes became scarce as diamonds.

Needless to say, I wasn't surprised when the phone rang and the crane company we had lined up was on the other end of the line canceling our reservation and saying they were headed to Louisiana. Soon after that phone call, our generator companies were on the line with similar news.

No cranes? No generators? No house.

We immediately began calling companies across the nation looking for what equipment would be available and found out just how expensive it is to find cranes and generators during a national emergency! We knew we would have to pay big bucks in order to have what we needed, but we weren't even sure we could find anything.

Finally, someone referred us to a company in Oklahoma who would be able to provide the exact type of cranes we needed. Although it was down to the wire, we also landed two generators that same week, just in time for the practice house competition.

We needed an enormous generator for each practice house to run all of the paint spray rigs, electric saws and drills—and we got ones that could do that and more! The generators, each at least the size of a VW bug, arrived on trailers and boasted 100-gallon diesel fuel tanks!

As you will recall, the Black team's house did not make it past the concrete, and time was called on it in about thirty minutes. Needless to say, the cost of that house's crane and generator made for their own record of sorts— earning the not-so-prestigious title of the most expensive and shortest large-equipment rental in history.

In the heat of the moment on the one remaining practice house, we had nailguns firing and drills whirling amid the roar of a gigantic air compressor and our super-powerful generator. The atmosphere was tense because with every passing hour, the finish line seemed further and further away. Mistakes, miscommunications and other distractions veered the project way off course. It was in that context of frenetic activity that one major detail got overlooked. But when it surfaced, it brought with it the kind of urgency that arrested everyone's attention immediately.

HURRICANE KATRINA LEFT US SCRAMBLING FOR A CRANE AT THE LAST MINUTE.

Don't misunderstand—the generators were essential to the project and they, along with the cranes, probably received more attention than anything else because it gave us quite a scare to think of losing them. However, we were using far more nailguns than anything else—tools fueled by an equally impressive trailer-mounted air compressor. We had allotted only so much fuel for a limited number of hours to be on the practice site. (After all, it was the "2 Hour" House project!)

Two hours in, work screeched to a halt as dozens of nailguns sputtered and wheezed to a standstill. The sudden eerie silence during what had up to that point had been a battleground of heavy nailgun fire spoke volumes to everyone on site about what had happened. We ran out of fuel.

Without a contingency plan for more diesel, we essentially cut ourselves off from going one minute longer once the last drop of diesel burned inside the compressor. We took our eyes off the big picture when we forgot more diesel. Everyone thought someone else had thought of that. No one had.

One of the most frustrating points about learning the Compressor Concept is that you often have to learn it the hard way! There was no way we could finish the house that day because of a multitude of issues. It wasn't going to happen.

However, I was disappointed that running out of gas meant we *had* to quit. It was beyond our control. And I didn't like the fact that we had unwittingly started that day without a way to finish right. (Fortunately, one of the guys had a diesel tank on his truck and we were able to continue.)

For us, this principle is a reminder that just when you think you have it all covered, go over it again. That final run through the details might just save the project from self-destructing.

> Just when you think you have it all covered, go over it again.

On a deeper level, it's also a lesson in what is important and not ignoring or overlooking what's important until it becomes a crisis! When we ran out of a simple thing like diesel, that one event resulted in a crisis moment and brought all of our other best efforts to a standstill.

Believe it or not, two weeks later on the day before the actual 2 Hour House event, we overlooked the compressor again! We were on the phone fifteen minutes prior to closing on Friday promising the rental shop we were on our way to get the compressor that no one had picked up earlier that day!

More than likely, there are issues in your family and/or business that represent aspects of the Compressor Concept. If you are not taking the time to refuel your most important relationships, you will soon know what I mean by learning this principle the hard way. If you are not giving your attention and leadership in a certain area at work that you're hoping will magically fix itself, before long you may have a crisis on your hands. These things often sneak up on you and catch you unaware, and the consequences are enormous.

Mastering the Details Raises Expectations

When people ask me if I ever want to get back into amateur racecar driving, I always say, "Not unless I could have my old crew back." Back in the day when I was driving for someone else, I could not wait for race day. We had a pre-race tradition that was unlike any other team on the track. Hours before the race, my crew and I would pull the car out to the track like every other crew did. However, instead of performing a triage of pre-race checks, we would set up a huge barbeque grill and start turning steaks.

Meanwhile, every other pit crew was racing around topping off tanks and tires and performing dozens of pre-race checklists while the smell of T-bones wafted just beyond their reach!

They even tried to call a meeting to kick us out of racing.

To be sure, we had the same checklists. The difference was that we made sure our crew had done our homework long before the time of the race arrived. We went over all the details ahead of time so that by the time we got out there, it was perfect. I wanted that racecar washed and looking brand new every time we pulled it off the trailer. And it did.

Sure, our steak-grilling and kick-back attitude drove our competitors crazy with envy. Not to mention the fact that we won nearly every championship we raced. I remember one year that some of the other drivers made stickers with our car's number and a line through it! They even tried to call a meeting to kick us out of racing. And I wasn't a dirty driver! Our only injustice was that we just got out there and won! Win after win, our attention to detail raised Cain but it also raised the expectations of every other crew out there. We seldom had a mechanical failure on the track.

In other words, details ensure quality control, no matter how you choose to accomplish them. By the time the 2 Hour House rolled around, we had developed an airtight system that categorized, analyzed and evaluated every detail throughout the house so that even the slightest deviation set off an alarm.

Mastering details in this way separated our crew of several hundred strong from any other housing crew in the nation and enabled us to do what no one else had done in over twenty years.

Mastering details is what separates good companies from better companies. Those who worked on the 2 Hour House knew what was expected of them. They also knew that everyone would be watching to see that they executed it perfectly.

Every committee member on the Quality Council had

THOSE WHO WORKED ON THE 2 HOUR HOUSE WERE HIGHLY MOTIVATED TO BE THE MOST PRODUCTIVE.

such dedication that they felt like their piece of the puzzle was the most important part of the entire project. They did not want to be the one who let everyone down. This kind of pressure had a positive effect on people that drove them to do their best.

It may seem like a large leap for a former racecar driver to go into the home-building business, but the two fields aren't that different. It takes a team working together in order to succeed. The driver gets all the glory when the checkered flag is raised, but there's an entire team behind him that got him to the finish line.

I never knew how to set up a car. I didn't want to know. I was just the driver—my job was to drive. The technician who works on the compressor is as important as the guy airing the tires, who is as important as the one under the hood cranking the last bit of juice that he can out of the engine. If one of the people on the pit crew doesn't do his job, the driver has a huge problem. Make that: the team has a huge problem.

At the 2 Hour House, it was race day. Everyone fed off each other's energy and dedication to the task; we all wanted it to succeed so that we could all set a world record.

Saying he drove for the 2 Hour House meant something beyond filling in blanks on an application.

I'll never forget a story Dick Schilhab told about one of the concrete truck drivers who later moved to another town. The manager from a trucking company in the new town called Dick one day as a routine check on the guy's references.

In the course of the conversation, the manager let Dick know an interesting thing about his application.

On it, the driver had written, "I drove for the 2 Hour House."

Don't tell that guy that his job that day (although brief in the big scheme of things) wasn't important. His sense of pride and ownership during the event was a result of raising the expectations for everyone who participated. For him to say he drove for the 2 Hour House meant something to that man beyond filling in blanks on an application.

And there are dozens of stories like his.

Those who worked on the 2 Hour House were highly

motivated to be the most productive. How do you get someone to understand the big picture and then be willing to do the least part in it and feel good about it? As the leader, that's your job.

The smallest detail handled by the least employee in the most effective way can make a huge difference. Raise the level of expectation so that they realize that the way they greet customers on the phone or in person is the most important task they can perform for the good of the company.

Treat the details of their jobs with importance, and you will see a difference in the behavior of your employees. For the 2 Hour House, that meant building a system that fit our people. And we had to have the right people who fit the system.

> Treat the details of their jobs with importance, and you will see a difference in the behavior of your employees.

I've heard pro football coaches talk about how a certain star player is "a great fit with our system." What he really means is that it's a combination of the right player and the right system. It's both/and, not either/or.

The system works well with the player's strengths and shores up his weaknesses. But the player also comes to the system with a skillset and attitude that can handle the expectations placed on him.

The result is a recipe for success.

RAISING THE ROOF

The roof was probably the most complicated web of details that had to come together. We planned to build the roof entirely separate from the house and hoist it with all of its materials intact, including thousands of shingles on top. A design had to be engineered that could withstand its own weight (30,000 pounds), yet also be lifted up in the air on a crane. Did I mention that the subdivision we chose was near an airport? There were very few trees to break the wind, and when the enormous roof was in the air, it had the potential to catch the wind like a sail and blow the entire crane over.

One mistake, and the roof section could crush the walls. A serious mistake and the entire roof itself could come crashing to the ground. At the right time, the crane precariously lifted the roof section into

CAREFULLY RAISING THE 30,000 POUND ROOF ONTO THE HOME.

the air and we made certain everyone cleared out of the way! The roof section for this 2249 square foot house weighed the equivalent of a semi-tractor trailer. Now imagine that swinging in mid-air with several hundred volunteers and spectators nearby.

There was no room for error.

To Think About

- How does mastering the details separate good companies from better ones?

- Are your people motivated to fulfill the goal down to the smallest detail? Why or why not?

- What can you do to avoid making false assumptions in your business?

- How is the principle of increasing speed without losing attention to detail at work in your business today?

- How do you relate to the lessons learned from the Compressor Concept?

- How have you seen attention to detail raise expectations in an organization?

NOTES

I learned that people who compete against each other every day in business can come together to set a world record. And they can do it for the good of the community.

Kevin H. Hester
Chairman
Drywall Committee

THE PRINCIPLE OF PERSISTENCE

There is no limit to what visionary leadership can accomplish

This book is about building leadership from the ground up. As you can see, the lessons learned from this experience could apply in a variety of contexts, at work and at home. The story of the 2 Hour House is unique, but the principles the story illustrates are not. They are fundamental leadership principles that apply to everyday life.

I believe that leadership is essential in areas that go far beyond building a building or our daily job. It is essential in any relationship, business or personal. Being an effective leader after five o'clock and a wise decision-maker at home is as important as being one at work. If you are a parent, you are a leader in your home as you set the example and guide your children.

This story is for anyone who ever had a dream of being more and doing more. If you have that dream, then you are beginning to realize that *doing more* will *take more*. More time. More energy. More patience. Beyond anything else, I'm convinced that our story turned out the way it did because of persistence. Anything worth doing takes persistence—giving more than you thought you could give. If you can hang in there when times are tough and you're not sure what to do next, it will get you one step closer to realizing your goals. As we got closer to realizing the world record, we were at a point where we had to give it all we had.

Roofing Issues

As workers finished out the interior walls, the roofers were about to go on stage. They'd had thirty minutes to assemble the entire roof, although we allowed them a little more than that to give enough time to plumb the walls and nail them together before we set the roof on top.

The framers began with the trusses (a triangle-shaped lattice-work of two-by-fours). A standard gable roof is the simplest arrangement, with gable end trusses at both ends and common

WE PRE-MEASURED EACH SLOT IN THE JIG TO MAKE SURE EACH TRUSS FIT PERFECTLY INTO PLACE.

trusses spaced in between. Gable end trusses sit on the end walls and carry the weight of the roof directly into the wall below. Common trusses are designed to offset the weight and span between the exterior walls.

A team of men carried each truss and set it into a jig—an open wood frame about five feet off the ground that held each piece of the roof snug. Each slot in the jig had been pre-measured so that each truss fit perfectly into place, allowing us to simply set and brace each one.

The jig or pony-wall was built high enough off the ground for men to crawl underneath and work on their knees underneath the roof section, feverishly tying in electrical wires, flextube plumbing and weaving in most of the HVAC system and duct work. In fact, it took a mere nine minutes to rough in the HVAC unit and components.

Before the roof would be placed on the house itself, it would have to have most of the necessary components wired and installed inside of it (not to mention the plywood decking and shingles on top), which would account for its tremendous weight.

One of the most difficult aspects of the roof was loading two extremely heavy beams through the center of the roof that would act as stabilizing bars for the entire roof. Each beam was four inches wide, 18 inches thick and over 40 feet long. Weighing 1200 pounds each, the two beams together were heavier than a typical four-door sports sedan. It was quite a sight to see over 50 guys hoist those beasts by hand and carefully thread each one down the center of the roof.

> One of the most difficult aspects of the roof was loading two extremely heavy beams through the center of the roof that would act as stabilizing bars for the entire roof.

At the same time, deckers were nailing the exterior of the roof with plywood decking, paper and the shingles. Dozens of nailguns sounded like automatic weapons firing as they precisely nailed section after section of roofing materials into place.

Finally, we strapped the roof section to the crane and tied extra ropes on the corners of the roof so we could swing and guide it by hand in order to make a precise drop onto the walls.

As the roof section gently came to rest, perfectly positioned on the corners of the walls, everyone breathed a sigh of relief.

We released the guide ropes. The crane operator maneuvered the massive arm back into position and slowly lumbered off the field, having completed its job in record time.

THE ROOF SECTION GINGERLY COMES TO REST AMID A CHEERING CROWD.

Because we had already installed all of the plumbing, wire and HVAC before it left the ground, the only thing we needed to do once the roof was secured to the frame of the house was to connect the plumbing and electrical wiring.

By design, much of the plumbing went overhead in the attic area in the 2 Hour House. This innovative technique was a series of flextubes wedged together in the ceiling instead of buried underneath in the foundation. (Only the sewer system was underneath the slab in this house.) They drilled holes for the tubes to connect to the tubes in the walls when they framed the walls. When the roof section met the frame section of the house, the holes had to align perfectly so that the only job left was to pull the tubes through the holes and connect the two together.

Like a surgeon reattaching a limb and carefully connecting veins and tiny capillaries together, each wire in the walls also had to match precisely to the wires in the roof, although the two were constructed several dozen yards away from each other by two entirely different crews.

The number of details at this point was exponential—the more we did, the more we had to do—but this is where what I call the power of participation came into play. The power of participation means not just adding people to the team, but increasing the effectiveness of those on the team.

THE POWER OF PARTICIPATION

Have you learned how several people thinking together can create another mind? This "mastermind," if you will, is able to run through a master list of details much faster and much easier than an individual can. It can also generate more and often better solutions to problems. It's another brain, a collective resource of smart thinking.

The power of participation increases effectiveness because of collaboration, but it matters *which* people you have on your team. You don't necessarily gain anything by just having more people. You have to have the *right* people and the right procedure to know how to most effectively use them. I like the motto of the New England Patriots who say, "It's not about collecting talent. It's about building a team."

This is exactly why I made a tough call on the concrete crews the day of the practice house. As you will recall, there were eight total crews that day; two worked on the failed Black team and six worked on the successful Red team. However, for the actual event itself, I only needed about 100 people on the slab and had to let the others go.

It was a crucial decision when I chose the "failed" Black team to serve on the 2 Hour House, and it was a controversial decision to say the least. Why in the world did I take two failed crews over six successful crews?

Why in the world did I take two failed crews over six successful crews?

First, the Black team's concrete had failed, but it was a miscommunication error outside of their control. So it wasn't a pass/fail decision. I wish it had been that easy!

Second, more manpower is not always the best solution to a problem. It can be tempting to match a bunch of details with a bunch of people. The six crews on the Red team had three times the number of eyes and hands to work the concrete issues. However, I wasn't interested in adding people to the team just to have more teammates.

Third, only the strongest ones with the right combination of assets would be able to execute the necessary details correctly. From my perspective, that was the Black team. A key piece of information I used in my decision was the fact that the six crews on the Red team had never worked together before that day. And it showed. They had six different "bosses" telling everyone what to do six different ways! However, the Black team had worked together on previous occasions and had established a team rhythm.

It was the right decision for the sake of the bigger picture, but it was hard for those on the successful Red team's concrete crews to understand. To make things even worse, not everyone on the six crews received the right information about the cancellation. One crew from the Red team actually showed up ready to work on the day of the 2 Hour House. I had to turn them down and send them away.

That was not a happy moment.

The power of participation meant that we took the strongest performers from both teams in every area—roof, drywall, plumbing, electricity—so that we would have the best of the best on the day of the event.

It surprises some people to learn that we were looking to take as few people as possible to get the job done. We were into multiplication, not addition when it came to developing our team. If we could multiply one person's effectiveness by multi-tasking, I would take that one person over two in a heartbeat.

Tom Utz, the Quality Council chairperson over plumbing, originally had 80 plumbers involved when there were two houses scheduled. However, he had to make tough calls on who would work the 2 Hour House, because he could only use about half of them efficiently. When asked how he made his decision, he said he took the ones who showed the most interest in the project and had attended the meetings. "And that did not mean taking the most qualified," he added. Some of the more qualified technicians blew off the meetings and planned to show up the day of the event with a hope and a prayer. However, Tom left them off the team roster and chose the ones with heart.

You've seen that principle at work in sports events like the Super Bowl. The whole team goes, but only their best players actually get to play the game. The coach gets to decide his own definition of "best." And that is for the sake of the entire team and provides the best chances of securing a win.

How do you determine who is dispensable and indispensable to your goals? And at what point does that happen? It doesn't mean they are not valuable players; they got you to a certain point. In our situation, we needed all of those concrete crews and all 80 of the plumbers to reach our goal of manning two houses. When we decided to go to just one house, the goals changed. It would have been fun for them, but detrimental to our goal to keep them on past the time they were needed.

> You must identify who the dispensable and indispensable players are. And you must determine at what point they make the transition on the team.

In other words, two decisions are involved, both equally important. You must identify who the dispensable and indispensable players are. And you must determine at what point they make the transition on the team.

Identifying who is not contributing to the best interest of your team enables you to make other decisions so much easier. As a leader, it's easy to get caught up in a people-pleasing mentality, but that can short-circuit your effectiveness and end up hurting the team at large. Determining the non-essential people in relation to accomplishing your goal means knowing whose opinion carries the most weight and whose does not. It helps you to know who needs your attention, time and resources and who cannot have it right now. It keeps you focused.

I knew I had the right participant when I saw electricians who had finished their jobs helping other tradespeople. I saw roofers who were finished roofing, but cleaning the windows on the front porch. Half of the concrete guys stepped in to help carry and set the walls. They were all looking and wanting to do more of the detail work.

By the way, all of the materials and many of the tools were donated for the 2 Hour House project. Well over 100 suppliers and contractors donated materials and labor for such things as the exterior siding and accessories, 30-year roofing shingles, all of the wallboard, breaker boxes, switches and other electrical equipment. The market value of the home was $125,000, including all of the donated appliances, too.

Talk about powerful participation. Everyone wanted to help cover the details because of the groundswell of enthusiasm. Even non-industry people wanted to help, including providing food for all of the volunteers and other aspects of the project, which could be several dozen gallons of coffee, donuts, pizzas or briskets at one sitting!

CALL TIME

All the while that the roof section workers were completing the decking and shingles, we neared completion on the interior of the home. In fact, when they finished the front gable of the roof, the interior was mostly completed. Outside the home, we were closing in fast as well.

We found a unique way to

COORDINATING HUNDREDS OF WORKERS AT ONE TIME.

shave hours off the garage door assembly. Workers assembled the entire garage door outside of the house. Once it was assembled to precise dimensions, the crew took it inside the garage and screwed it into place. About 90 seconds later, what is typically a three-hour project was already complete.

The landscapers were a crew 80 strong, representing several companies. Some had doubts as to why the lot needed to be landscaped. To some it seemed like an unnecessary addition to the list of things to do! But to us that was just part of going beyond the limits of what others thought could be done. It was going the extra mile that we didn't have to go. Maybe it harkens back to my early days as a kid with my landscaping business (which I still own today incidentally), but a home is not complete if it doesn't have a yard, flowerbeds and a tree. It was important to me to do it all the way.

With the majority of workers still laboring inside, it opened up an opportunity for this massive landscaping crew to roll out sod throughout the front yard, dig flowerbeds and fill them with bushes and flowers as well as plant a tree and even put up a small fence. They waited patiently until the traffic flow had died down enough outside so they could roll sod without it being trampled on by hundreds of people! This last detail came at a clutch point on the time clock, but it was their moment to shine. And they did not let us down.

> This last detail came at a clutch point on the time clock, but it was their moment to shine.

In the remaining moments before official time was called on the 2 Hour House, we were making sure everything was in place. And I mean everything. We put in the dryer vent. We wiped counters and windows and swept away loads of trash.

I'll never forget my friend Carey getting on the bullhorn and barking out, "We need a doorbell over here for the front door asap!"

We didn't leave anything out...not even a doorbell.

I think that scene perfectly portrays our dedication to the task. It showed the spectators and crews that we would not let anything stand in the way of finishing the task.

Does your company have what you might call a Doorbell Directive? That extra touch that symbolizes your willingness to do more than what others might expect? It's something to consider, if you want to test what your leadership can accomplish.

PAINTING THE TRIM ON THE FRONT DOOR—NO DETAIL WAS OVERLOOKED.

For us, that idea meant that we were dedicated beyond what we had to be. We had created a culture of dedication to winning in every way, where the last minute touches we put on the house to make it a home counted as much as the foundation and roofing.

We would not have finished if something was missing. We did not want to lose track of a single piece.

When it became obvious that there were finally more workers outside the workzone than inside of it, everyone sensed the end was near. The crowd was on its feet cheering and clapping. People were hugging and high-fiving each other. I daresay there may have been some tears of exhaustion and disbelief on some of the rough, weather-worn faces that day. The chief inspector issued a certificate of occupancy for the 2249 square foot, 3 bedroom, 2 bath house and officially called the time at 2:52:29.

Two hours, fifty-two minutes and twenty-nine seconds. The world record had now been set.

PERSISTENCE PAYS

I smile when I remember what my friend Brad recalls about those last few weeks leading up to the project. "Brian—that guy, he never let up or gave up. Three weeks from the date of the 2 Hour House, I had given up. I had thrown in the towel. I was overwhelmed by the task at hand and the responsibility to keep my business running at the same time. We had so much buy in from the community and from our peers...so much pressure. Brian had to stay positive and upbeat—and he did."

> The magnitude of our mission continued to prompt us day and night to keep going despite the pain and confusion.

The magnitude of our mission continued to prompt us day and night to keep going despite the pain and confusion. Abraham Lincoln once remarked about the human spirit's capacity to persevere. "The sense of obligation to continue is present in all of us. A duty to strive is the duty of us all."

American history is full of leaders like Lincoln who continued to strive despite turmoil and who did not give up in the face of adversity. However, his story is unique in several respects because of his humble beginning as a young boy born in poverty who set his sights on politics. He faced defeat at many turns and lost several elections before becoming one of the greatest presidents our country has ever known at one of the most crucial times in our nation's history.

If you've ever studied Lincoln's road to the Whitehouse, it is clear that his was an uphill battle.

1816	His family was forced out of their home. He had to work to support them.
1818	His mother died.

1831	Failed in business.
1832	Ran for state legislature—lost.
1832	Also lost his job—wanted to go to law school but couldn't get in.
1833	Borrowed some money from a friend to begin a business and by the end of the year was bankrupt. He spent the next 17 years of his life paying off this debt.
1834	Ran for state legislature again—won.
1835	Was engaged to be married, sweetheart died and his heart was broken.
1836	Had a total nervous breakdown and was in bed for six months.
1838	Sought to become speaker of the state legislature—defeated.
1840	Sought to become elector—defeated.
1843	Ran for Congress—lost.
1846	Ran for Congress again—this time he won—went to Washington and did a good job.
1848	Ran for re-election to Congress—lost.
1849	Sought the job of land officer in his home state—rejected.
1854	Ran for Senate of the United States—lost.
1856	Sought the Vice-Presidential nomination at his party's national convention—got less than 100 votes.
1858	Ran for U.S. Senate again—again he lost.
1860	Elected president of the United States.

-Source unknown

MAKE THAT MONDAY MORNING PHONE CALL

Think about what would have happened if Lincoln's story had stopped after one of those low periods. I can't help but relate to his struggles because it's hard to come back from one failure, but several in a row? That's enough to crush anyone's spirit.

I know in our case that making a comeback after not one

but two failures with the practice houses tested our will. But it remains one of the best examples of how the principle of persistence works in real life. Some of the most difficult phone calls I've ever had to make took place the Monday after the practice house. I knew I had to rally the troops out of their defeat and depression, and in doing so, it strengthened my resolve to finish what we started.

Sometimes the best thing that will help you pull out of a nosedive is to take a deep breath and make that "Monday morning phone call." Do whatever you must do to keep going. I don't know what that means for you in your professional or personal life. It may be calling a meeting with your staff and discussing changes that need to happen in your business. It may be beating a deadline. Or going back to the drawing board on a concept. It may be a conversation you need to have, a lunch you need to schedule or a meeting you've been putting off. Whatever it takes to go forward with what you know is the right and best thing to do, do it.

> Whatever it takes to go forward with what you know is the right and best thing to do, do it.

LEARNING THE DIFFERENCE

After losing the Senate race, Lincoln said, "The path was worn and slippery. My foot slipped from under me, knocking the other out of the way, but I recovered and said to myself, 'It's a slip and not a fall.'"

It's all a matter of perspective.

A slip is a temporary setback. It gives us the valuable opportunity to rethink, reevaluate and try again—this time with more wisdom than before. I'm grateful for every slip we had during the 18 months of this experience.

Something that you consider to be a fall is usually fatal to your hopes and dreams. Not because of the circumstances, but because of your attitude about the circumstances. It's hard to recover from what you look at as a fall. Many people fail because they start with loads of enthusiasm and yet it soon fizzles. Especially when problems arise. If they finish at all, they usually finish halfheartedly.

Or, I've seen situations where people overreact to a perceived failure and go back to the drawing board time and time again. Sometimes we get a little gun shy because we made a mistake. In order to keep from making another mistake, we want to delay taking the hill or reaching the finish line until we've "thought about it some more."

Leaders like that suffer from the paralysis of analysis when things go wrong. I guess we could have delayed the 2 Hour House three to six months when we had such a fiasco with the practice house. We could have taken that time to work out all the kinks and perfect it in the lab once more.

If your desire is strong enough, and your plans flexible enough, you can accomplish anything you set your mind to do.

However, we only had two weeks—just enough time to move forward and not talk ourselves out of it!

What Churchill said to inspire the English people who were facing an invasion from a brutal enemy during World War II is inspiring. He didn't know *how* they would achieve victory over the Germans necessarily; he just knew they would never give up.

"We shall not flag nor fail. We shall go on to the end. We shall fight in France and on the seas and oceans; we shall fight with growing confidence and growing strength in the air. We shall defend our island, whatever the cost may be, we shall fight on the beaches, we shall fight on the landing grounds, we shall fight in the fields and in the streets, we shall fight in the hills; we shall never surrender," Winston Churchill, June 4, 1940.

I believe that everything you want to do in life starts with a desire then follows with a plan. If your desire is strong enough, and your plans flexible enough, you can accomplish anything you set your mind to do.

You just cannot give up on the dream or on yourself.

NEVER GIVE UP ON PEOPLE

It was an accomplishment in itself that we beat our practice house time by more than half—a mere two weeks later. However, I still think I could shave a good 30 minutes off our record today if we had another shot at it!

However, I'm not saying that we would save time primarily because of what I learned about the system that we built and the tweaks we could make to it. I think we could break our own record again today primarily because of what I learned about *the people* who worked our system.

I now know more about their strengths and what they bring to the table. I know more about what they're capable of doing... and I like to think that they do, too. The vision I had in my mind throughout this project was not a compilation of bricks and mortar.

WE DIDN'T JUST BUILD A HOUSE. WE BUILT PEOPLE WHO BELIEVED IN THEMSELVES.

I had the faces of the people who would be working with and among us in mind.

We didn't even finish the first time we did the practice house. And this time, we finished as a team! I'm convinced that one of the secrets to our success was that we never gave up on our people. We knew they could do it; sometimes our job was just to convince themselves of that fact.

Interestingly, as the president of our association, I was surprised how many inactive and uninvolved members of our association got turned on by this project. Something drew them out of their complacency when this project came along, and I believe it was the lure of a challenge. Nothing had challenged them like this and motivated them to do something with the other members. We basically threw something out there that was so crazy that for the first time they wanted to be involved.

I am a builder by profession, but I learned that I am building a lot more than I realized.

As a result of everyone's efforts, we won the 2005 Association Excellence award from the Texas Association of Builders for the 2 Hour House project—a builders group with a membership over 11,000 people strong!

PEOPLE MATTER

Today, whenever someone asks me why I did this, I return to my three initial goals: 1) to set a record 2) to bring our community together and 3) to raise money for charities. We were able to do all three, and all three dealt with people at their core. Some people started calling the 2 Hour House "The House That Tyler Built," and that is an excellent description of what happened. Early on, the decision was made not to limit the participation in the 2 Hour House only to members of our association. We wanted to share this opportunity to set a record with everyone who wanted to be a part of it. The City of Tyler was very involved at all of the meetings and helped us the entire way.

I've said many times that world records like ours will come and go, especially as technology continues to improve and men and women continue to dream dreams! But the friendships among those who served and the impact on our community will last a lifetime.

Anyone who worked on the 2 Hour House in any capacity could not help but be changed by the experience. I learned a good deal about myself in the process.

I am a builder by profession, but I learned that I am building a lot more than I realized. At work, I am building people all the time. At home, I'm building my children into confident and capable adults.

In the midst of building a house, we were able to build people up by causing them to believe in themselves. Raising the bar of their performance and stretching them to do something beyond what they'd ever imagined built confidence. Sometimes it hits me all over again that what we did, we did with volunteers. Not paid professionals. In my mind, the sacrifice of time this project took away from their regular jobs and families makes their accomplishment that much more significant.

> At work, I am building people all the time.

Where in your personal and professional life are you stretching yourself so much that you are risking it all? That's the time and place for real growth. Grow people by stretching them and entrusting big things to them that they think they cannot do for the simple pleasure that is its own reward—success.

Above all, the 2 Hour House experience gave all of us a precious gift. It is something I can pass on to my children and their children that will mean more to them than any tangible inheritance. It is the belief that everything is possible. Everything.

Sometimes life brings daunting doubts, real fears and many uncertainties our way. I know my kids will face challenges in their lifetimes that seem so overwhelming that they may be tempted to give up. Like everyone else, they will encounter chances to do what they think they don't have the courage to do. And if they listen to those who say they're crazy for considering it, they'll miss those chances, one by one. However, my greatest hope is that they will remember this story.

And believe.

TO THINK ABOUT

- In what areas of your life right now do you need to practice more persistence?

- What are you learning about the strengths and weaknesses of your colleagues, friends, family?

- What opportunities do you have to build people up throughout your day?

- How do you see the power of participation at work in your company— not just adding people to the team but increasing their effectiveness?

NOTES

This experience allowed me to fine tune my company's efficiency and create procedures that maximize productivity. No doubt, it remains the single most impressive project I have ever been a part of. Conaway's vision for success has broadened my expectations for excellence. Nothing is impossible.

Carey Crist
Executive Board, OSHA Safety and Hardware

My job was pretty simple: to design an efficient home that took all aspects of construction into consideration, including the simplicity of the roof structure, location of the plumbing fixtures, doors, windows, walls, etc. The design only took a couple of weeks to create. However, I was amazed to see how a minor problem had the potential to threaten the whole project. One little negative pulled the attention away from all of the positives. Even though each minor problem was a drop in the bucket, the waves it created could pull our focus away from all the good that we had done. I learned that it's more important to focus on the positives and work around the negatives than it is to fixate on the negatives without the ability to move forward with the positives.

Brent Conaway
2 Hour House Designer

Anything can be accomplished by coordination, organization and planning. With the media and community watching, everyone had to keep their cool, stay motivated and know their responsibilities. We realized that we could finish on time only if we worked together. It's true—teamwork works.

Eric Dorsey
Chairman, Framing Committee

This was one of the most powerful projects that I have ever been a part of. The leadership was so inspiring, and I learned a great deal from it. The entire community came together and worked toward this tremendous goal and we achieved it! It was the experience of a lifetime…something people will talk about many, many years from now.

Jennifer Eckles
Chairman, Marketing and Sponsorship

Characteristics like motivation and organization, dedication and leadership made an impact on my life and were crucial in bringing many people of all backgrounds together to accomplish one goal. Being a part of such an amazing accomplishment has reminded me that without teamwork, we would all fail.

Jason Eschberger
Materials Coordinator

This project brought my installation department together and demonstrated to them that with a designated plan and teamwork, they can achieve the impossible. The entire HVAC system was installed in under 15 minutes!

Todd Green
Chairman, HVAC Committee

I learned that anything is possible if you put your mind to it. This project taught me that it's not one person who is the key, but it's everybody working together as a team.

Ryan Hall
Materials Coordinator, Staging

Having all the different trades come together to work as a team was a joy to see. Competitors put aside their differences and worked toward a common goal that benefited the community.

Greg Kirkley
Chairman, Food/Beverage Committee

After a failed practice house, there were serious doubts. However, when the gun went off to signal the start of the 2 Hour House, things went smoothly. For the first time, everyone really believed we could accomplish the house in the timeframe. What's really amazing to me is how the suppliers, contractors and builders worked side by side to make this house possible.

Jimmy Martin
Chairman, Dry Wall Committee

We all have the ability to overcome what sometimes seems to be impossible. At my first meeting with the Garage Door Team, I had the luxury of informing them that the garage door would need to be installed in less than three minutes. They looked at me like I was crazy. We all left that meeting feeling apprehensive. A week later, I checked in with them to see how the planning process was going. They informed me that they had developed a system, tested it and could now get a functioning door installed in 90 seconds with a team of six. My jaw dropped. What seemed impossible was now a reality and could be accomplished well within our goal.

Chris Moore
Chairman, Garage Door Committee

This project was a very rewarding experience in our efforts to gather community support. It was an opportunity to work with other local professionals and develop lasting friendships.

Shane Payne
Chairman, Video Production Committee

We learned that the best made plans are worthless if you do not follow up with organized, structured practice and lots of it. You really can leave no stone unturned when planning and communicating. The most important thing that we learned was that no matter how challenging the task, with the proper leadership and a shared vision, any group can accomplish a dream and overcome many roadblocks.

Dick Schilhab
Foundation/Concrete Committee

Few places in society (outside of the sports arena) see more competitive spirits and egotism than in the construction trade. To collect the talent and skill needed to build this house is one thing—to manage it while observing an incredibly tight time-frame is remarkable. Only a can-do attitude and optimism could lead to a successful meeting of goals in this undertaking.

Sam Vercher
Chairman, Tape and Bed Committee

SPECIAL THANKS
The 2 Hour House Volunteers

Task Force Chairmen

Robert Aiken
Chris Baker
Renee Bennett
Miles Brosang
Keith Carter
Brent Conaway
Carey Crist

Eric Dorsey
Jennifer Eckles
Shane Fisher
Todd Green
Scott Greene
Steve Herber
Kevin Hester

Randy Humphrey
Anwar Khalifa
Greg Kirkley
Kevin Koop
Jimmy Martin
Chris Moore
Cherie' Paro

Shane Payne
Jesse Rider
Brad Root
Ron Troxell
Tom Utz
Sam Vercher
Debra Ward

Sponsors

A.O. Smith Water Heaters
AAA Sanitation
Alan Utz and Associates
All American Party and Tent Rental
All Natural Grass & Stone
Allied Truss Mfg.
Alpha Pest Control Co.
Altra Federal C.U.
Ameritex Services, Inc.
Apex Geoscience
Arp State Bank
Ashcraft Marble Co, Inc.
Atco Rubber Products
Bannister Drywall
Barrett Appliance Distributors
Barrett Graphics
Berry Marble And Granite
Black Jack Roll Off
Blackstone Irrigation
Bobby Reece Construction
Booth Roofing
Brandom Cabinets
Brass Craft
Breedlove Nursery
Brian Ashby Plumbing
Brookshires
Brosangs Landscaping
BSCENE Magazine
Builders Carpet & Design Center, Inc.
Building Savvy

Buttram Plumbing
C. Woods Co., Inc.
Cassity Jones - Tyler
Cavenders Boot City
C.C. Drywall
Center Point Energy
Charles Breedlove Nursery
Charlotte Pipe & Foundry Co.
Choice One Realty,
Donald & Mindy Smith
City Of Tyler
City Of Tyler Solid Waste
Coburns Supply Co.
Coldwell Banker United, Robin Liles
Consolidated Plumbing Industries
Coors Of Longview
COX Communications
COX Media
Custom Landscape
Dairy Queen
Darryl Bonner Electric
David Cooper Construction
Dearborn Brass Co.
Design Center Signs & Banners
Designer Graphics
Designing Women, Inc.
Dons TV & Appliances, Inc.
Dorsey Homes
Double Daves Pizza
East Texas Automation
East Texas Door Co., Inc.
East Texas Medical Center

East Texas Refrigeration, Inc.
East Texas Staple
Elkay Manufacturing Co.
Envirocare
Family Plumbing
First Horizon Home Loans
Fisher Construction
Fixture This, Inc.
Food Fast #57
Fountain Plumbing
Garland Insulating, Inc.
Gillian and Harold Brasfield
Gilpin Roofing
Glow In The Dark Productions
Dan Velie & Robin Liles
Golden Brook Ice Cream
Granite Loc
Gregory Real Estate, Emily Smith
Group M7
Hamilton Supply
Heather Hughey
HOBO Construction
Holey Plumbing
Holiday Inn Select
Holland Marble
Home and Garden Resource Directory
Home Plus
Homes and Land Magazine
Hudson Printing and Graphic Design
Hughes Plant Farm
InnerSpace Custom Storage Solutions
Insulation Supply Co.
Insurance One Agency, L.L.C.
Ivy Plumbing
J&W Roofing
Jan Payne
Jerry Black Plumbing
Jerry Vandergriff Plumbing
Josephs Catering
Julians Asian Diner
Katie Wallace
KBLZ
KETK Channel 56
KLTV Channel 7
KYTX Channel 19
KNUE
KOOI
KTBB

KTYL
Lamar Advertising Company
Larry Blalock Landscape
Lasco Bathware
Leo Jones Insulating Co., Inc.
Luckett Crane
M&M Manufacturing
Matt Drywall
McClain Wholesale
Danvid Windows
McCoy's
McIntyre Plumbing
Med Safe
Millican Maintenance
Mink Plumbing Co., Inc.
Miracle Plumbing
Montrose Concrete
Moore Supply
Morrison Supply
Moyer Plumbing Company
Nichiha Capital
Oatey Svcs.
Overhead Door Company of Tyler
Panel Truss Texas, Inc.
Papacitas
Paul & Shannon Hildreth
Perry Hall Homes
Planet Landscape
Price Pfister Faucet Co.
Priddy Drywall
R&K Distributors
Re/Max, Doug Crutcher & P.J. Hartley
Real Estate Center of East Texas
Reeves Drywall
Residence Inn
Rosenbergs Outdoor Designs
Rudd Plumbing
Selkirk Metalbestos
Sensible Sign Company
Shaw Industries
Sherwin Williams
Showcase of Homes
Southwest Commercial Contractors
Spivey Concrete
Standard Coffee Services
Sugar Mountain Design Company
Super 1 Foods
Temple-Inland

SPECIAL THANKS

The Blind Place Tyler
The Granite Girls
Trane Co.
Transit Mix
Troxell Custom Paint
Tuckers Liquor Store
Twenty East Agency L.L.C.
TXU Energy
Tyler Area Chamber Of Commerce
Tyler Beverage
Tyler Golf Carts, Inc.
Tyler Hotel/Motel Association

Tyler Morning Telegraph
Tyler Pest Services, Inc.
United Plumbing Company
United Rentals
Vitra USA, Inc.
Waterman Construction
Watson Plumbing, Inc.
Watts Regulator Co.
Weatherization Partners (TYVEK)
Wellington Place
Wilhite Landscaping
Woodland Builders

Team Members

Reuben Abilaneda
Justin Adams
Daniel Agullar
Leon Agulrre
Robert Aiken
Isidro Alredondo
Hermen Alejo
Chad Alexander
Lorry Allen
Jeff Almond
Alex Alonzo
Baldemar Alvarado
Edgar Alvarado
Mark Amaril
Dalton Anderson
Rolando Aparicio
Trino Aparicio
Jason Arbuckle
Reynoldo Arellano
Jeronimo Arfilo
Angel Argote
Apollnar Argote
Jose Argote
Oscar Arieaga
Charles Ashcraft
Jason Ashcraft
Richard Ashmore
Weldon Atherton
Ector Avila
Genaro Aviles
Francisco Ayala
Jose Ayglcu

Chad Azbell
Chris Baker
Cody Baker
Lonnie Baker
Gusfovo Balalcios
Renee Balderas
Alfredo Balderes
Mitch Baldwin
Ingacio Baluvenis
Danny Banks
Brandon Bannister
Cecil Bannister
Octavio Bardagan
Michael Barnett
Tommy Barnhart
Jorge Barrera
Alicia Barrett
Hector Barrios
Pam Bates
Jose Bautista
Faye Baxter-Jones
David Beall
Chris Bearden
Shannon Bearden
Bob Beckley
Jonathan Beeler
Nicky Bell
Robert Bemis
Jerry Benavides
Miguel Benitez
Rogello Benitez
Thomas Benitez
Cody Bennett

Troy Bevill
Kenneth Bickham
Sheila Billingsley
Cory Bishop
Gary Black
Jeff Blackstone
Malgen Blackstone
Larry Blalock
Andy Blas
Faye Bobbitt
Hinio Bocanegia
Steven Boggs
Jerry Bonavides
Gayla Bonavides
Ben Bonner
Danny Bonner
Bonnie Booker
David Booker
Robert Bowens
Mike Boyd
Gillian Brasfield
John Braun
Zeb Browner
Jeff Brewer
Brand Bridges
Cody Brooks
Jerry Brooks
Michael Brosang
Miles Brosang
Billy Brown
Kim Brown
Shaun Brown
Fred Browning

SPECIAL THANKS

Sandra Browning
Danny Bryant
Dexter Bullington
Brandon Burgess
Eva Burner
Rex Buttram
Salvador Campuzano
Tony Canfield
Mary Cantrell
Roberta Capuzano
Johnny Carnahan
Joyce Carney
Martha Camey
Mike Carpenter
Angel Carranza
Domingo Carreno
Jerry Carter
Keith Carter
Beverly Casey
Ricky Casey
Dolph Cason
Juan Castaneda
Juvenfino Castaneda
Jason Castro
Clint Chambers
Bryan Chapman
Cecil Chapman
Patrick Charping
Shannon Childress
Jake Chilek
Bruce Christianson
Andy Christopher
Robbie Claiborne
James Clark
Johnny Clark
Day Clemmer
Brandon Cochran
Freddy Codillo
Noe Codillo
Amber Coby
Mark Coby
Mark Colby
Lynette Paro Colglazier
Brenda Conine
Jose Contreras
Eugene Cook
James Cook
Porter Cook

David Cooper
Steve Cooper
Arturo Corsica
Arisme Cornelia
Rigaberto Cornelio
Crecencelo Corona
Victor Coronado
Rick Cotton
Greg Courtney
Boyd Cox
Becky Craft
Kristi Crenshaw
Clayton Crews
John Crimes
Kevin Cruise
Antonio Cruz
Israel Cruz
Miguel Cruz
Jeff Crymes
Keith Cubbit
Billy Dalley
Andre Daniel
Jerry Davis
Terry Davis
Steven Deaton
Doug Debusk
Alan Delacruz
Albert Delacruz
Tony Dockery
Jueniino Domaro
Lenin Dominguez
Eric Dorsey
Tony Dorsey
Randy Dougherty
Dona Dudley
Haul Dulun
Amy Duquette
Antonio Duran
Ellceo Duran
Erasmo Duran
Aaron Eaton
Brad Eaton
Effran Escabado
Mollna Esdeban
Juan Espladola
Juan Carlos Espinoza
Mersedes Estrada
Tom Evans

Andy Faggard
Gary Fain
Michael Farnham
Jason Farrell
Danny Feagins
Johnny Fernandez
Randy Feuerhelm
Shane Fisher
Kevin Fitts
Robert Fletcher
Uoyd Flores
Kevin Folsom
Larkin Forman
Rick Forman
Darrell Foster
Kevin Fountain
Dale Fowler
Diana Frachiseur
Bryan Free
Eric Free
Ryan Frost
Mando Fuentes
Steve Galvan
Ramon Galvez
Kim Galyean
Ellsender Gama
Francisco Garcia
Joel Garcia
Miguel Garcia
Al Gregory
Chuck Gregory
Cindy Gregory
Gene Griffin
Tommy Griffin
Steve Griffith
Miguel Guerrera
Judith Guthrie
Marshall Guthrie
Max Gutterrez
Ed Hacker
Richard Hagan
Dale Halbert
Randy Hale
Ryan Hall
Heath Hallmark
Joe Hamilton
Joe Hancock
Wilton Hancock

Shawn Haney
Michael Hanna
Dee Dee Hanson
Richard Harris
Sedric Harris
Michaela Harris
Teresa Harris
Xavier Harris
Zachary Harris
Tracy Harrison
Adrian Hart
Marshall Hart
Stephen Harvey
Kimberly Hawkins
Bryce Hayes
Randy Hayes
Todd Hayley
Matt Henderson
Rod Henderson
Steve Herber
Antonio Hemandes
Arturo Hernandez
Gustavo Hernandez
Israel Hernandez
Israias Hernandez
Joel Hernandez
Jose Hernandez
Luis Hernandez
Manuel Hernandez
Miguel Hernandez
J.D. Hester
Jody Hester
Kevin Hester
Laiaro Heuveria
Andrew Hicken
Scott Hilburn
Carrie Hill
Ron Hill
Tony Hill
Carl Hiltpold
Celia Hinson
Katherine Hogue
Neal Hague
Frank Holey
John Holey
Catherine Holiday
Josh Holland
Ronnie Holley

Kim Holman
Stacy Holman
Mike Hoover
Dave Howell
Berigno Huerta
Javier Huerto
Chris Hukill
Gerardo Ibarra
Joel Ibarra
Manuel Ibarra
Jaime Ibarro
Keith Intlehouse
Keith Isaac
Dennis Ivy
Chad Jackman
Adam Jaimes
Jose Jaimes
Felip James
Alfonso Janez
Pemeetrio Jarmillo
Alien Jennings
David Jennings
Abelardo Jimenez
Terry Jernigan
Chris Jeter
Keith Jeter
Dave Jewell
Joshua Johnson
Todd Johnson
Clifton Johnston
Joseph R. Johnston
Kody Johnston
David Jones
James Jones
Michael Jones
Leo Jones, Jr.
Christopher Joseph
Antheimo Juarez
Michael Kemper
Jason Key
Anwar Khalifa
Debra King
Odel King
Aaron Kinser
Patty Kirkpatrick
Lorry Kitchens
Tim Kitchens
Robert Knight

Frank Knox
Diana Koop
Kevin Koop
Matthew Koop
Jake Kovarik
Chad Lackey
Anthony Langdon
James Langdon
Jessica Lanphear
Lucretia Lanphear
Travis Leahy
Stephen Lear
Larry Leathers
Scott Lee
Pam Leger
Mark Lemley
Amy Lennon
Scott Lewis
Antonio Leyva
Robin Liles
Rafael Llanes
Robert Lloyd
Toby Loden
Tracy Logan
Russell Logsdon
Jimmy Lollar
Melvin Lollar
Fernando Lopez
Kevin Loudamy
Tony Loudamy
Eric Lowe
Larry Lowe
Ross Lowrance
Hernado Luveno
Luvlano Luveno
Stephen Luveno
Samuel Macias
Keith Madigan
Wade Mahon
Danny Makowsky
Darlen Makowsky
Janie Malone
Jerry Mann
Robert Marguez
Darrin Martin
Eric Martin
James Martin
Jimmy Martin

Keith Martin
Mary Ann Martin
Aristo Martinez
Gustavo Martinez
Hector Martinez
Ivan Martinez
Job Martinez
Jorge Martinez
Omar Martinez
Roberta Martinez
Wilverdo Martinez
Adrian Mata
Arturo Mata
Hugo Mata
Joe Mata
Joel Mata
Jose Mata
Michael Matthews
Robby Maxfield
Pam Mayfield
Danny Mayo
Jennie Mayo
Tommy McAlester
Craig McAlister
Amanda McAnally
Casey McAnally
Debra McAtee
Danny McCall
Harriet McCoy
Jerry Don McCuin
Charles McIntyre
Josh McKeever
Robert McKenzle
Robin McKenzle
Katrina McNell
Zack McNew
Darrell McQueen
Frank McQueen
Stacey Mead
Rusty Meadville
Efrian Mederos
Joel Francisco Medina
Luis Melendez
Tony Melton
Umberto Mendoza
Mike Merton, Jr.
Mark Miears
Jimmy Miles

Joe Miller
Becky Millican
Shane Millican
Benny Mills
Wendy Minix
Ed Mink
Lee Mink
Shelby Mink
Nickey Minyard
Shannon Minyard
Donnie Mitchell
Denny Mize
Rugoberto Mojarro
Blu Monday
Angel Monsivais
Joshua Montrose
Larry Montrose
Jeremy Moore
Jesse Moore
Jimmy Moore
Eddy Moose
Harold Moose
Joel Morales
Ray Morales
Gonzalo Moreno
Gerald Morgan
Donald Morris
Shane Morris
Mike Mosley
Ray Mosley
Nick Moss
Jesus Munos
Cesar Munoz
Jose Munoz
Rigo Munoz
Riso Munoz
Tranavillo Murillo
Cheryl Murphy
Jason Myers
Ron Narvaez
Ron Nelson
Seaborn Nesbitt
Troy Neuman
Ben Nevill
Jason Newport
Paula Nichols
Shelly Nichols
Diane Nicholson

Rodney Hootie Nix
Gylly Noriega
Jose Noyla
David O'Brien
Jaime Onueta
Gregorio Orozco
Pablo Orozco
Pete Ortega
Mark Overlender
Walter Overstreet
Mike Owen
Tenri Owen
E. Fred Pacheco
Hugo Palacios
Jaime Palacios
Joel Palacios
Leah Parker
Chris Parks
Joyce Paro
Joe Partin, Jr.
Sandra Pastrona
Paul Patterson
Jan Payne
Steve Payne
Roque Penaloza
Santiago Penaloza
Bill Pennington
Carlos Perdomo
Jose Perdomo
Jose Juan Perdomo
Jaime Pereira
Censor Perez
Jimmie Perez
Jose Perez
Jose Pepe Perez
Roger Perez
Saul Perez
Greg Perkins
Jill Peters
Todd Peterson
Robert Petterson
Barbara Phillips
Ben Phillips
Durwood Phillips
Noe Pineida
Kirn Pizzola
Alfonso Ponce
Joshua Poston

SPECIAL THANKS

Larry Powell
Paul Priddy
Samuel Priddy
Buddy Pringle
Edwardo Ramarez
Jesus Ramerez
Chris Ramirez
Edwin Ramirez
Luis Ramirez
Noe Ramirez
Aburto C. Ramulto
Jesus Rautista
Peggy Ray
Renee Ray
Eduordo Rayo
Shane Reaves
Bobby Reece
Cedric Reeves
Terrence Reeves
Manuel Rendon
Roger Renteria
Heidi Ressmann
Kirk Ressmann
Lindsey Ressmann
Felipe Reyes
Francisco Reyes
Jose Reyes
Miguel Reyes
John Reynolds
Mike Richards
Vicente Ricin
Jake Rider
Rob Risko
Felipe Rivas
Luis Rivera
Steve Roach
Wes Roach
Jerry Robertson
Peter Robertson
Scott Robertson
Albertico Rocha
Antonio Rodriguez
Beto Rodriguez
Comello Rodriguez
Hugo Rodriguez
Jaime Rodriguez
Juan Rodriguez
Rene Rodriguez

Rolando Rodriguez
William Rodriguez
Gilberto Rodriquez
Ramon Rodriquez
Jose Rojas
Susie Roll
Benjamin Romero
Jennifer Romines
Robert Romines
Brad Root
David Roquemore
Corneleo Rosano
Gary Rosas
Louis Rosas
Nick Rosenburg
Greg Ross
Justin Ross
Kristi Ross
Bobby Rowland
Ruperto Rublo
Y. Fredy Ruiz
Jason Rushing
Crystal Russell
Carlos Salazar
Elias Salazar
Marguez Salomon
Vasquez Salvadore
Antotlon Sanchez
Evarista Sanchez
Fernando Sanchez
Gabriel Sanchez
Jose J.Sanchez
Julio Sanchez
Thomas Sanchez
Jaime Sandaval
Keith Sanders
Sissy Sanders
Juan Sanjez
Anteimo Santiago
Walter Scoggins
Willie Scott
Otero Sefranio
Jamie Selby
Tamie Jo Selby
Saul Serna
Miguez Serrano
Rafa Serrano
Roberta Serrano

Justin Settegast
Robert Shaw
Bobby Shepherd
Roger Shipley
Hannah Simmons
Jay Simmons
Katie Simmons
Caries Simon
Melissa Simpson
James Slaughter
Chris Small
Austin Smith
Brad Smith
Denny Smith
Eddie Smith
Emily Smith
Johnny Smith
Leonard Smith
Matthew Smith
Stefani Smith
Bobby Smotherman
Enrique Sotelo
Angel Soto
Jose Soto
Chris Spain
Eugene Spivey
Bryas Staley
Brittany Stanfill
Danny Stanfill
Jason Stanley
Marcia Starling
Clayton Steen
Sandy Stewart
Spencer Stokes
Terry Story
Jake Stout
Ben Stovall
Mary Strand
Jack Stringer
Josh Stubblefield
Alejandro Suarez
Miguel Suarez
Gerald Swindell
Kristin Tallent
Brandon Tannery
Cassandra Taylor
Curtis Toylor
Jeff Taylor

SPECIAL THANKS

Robert Taylor
Ron Taylor
Todd Taylor
Alien Terrell
Chad Thomas
James Thomas
Scott Thomas
Carly Thompson
Charlie Thompson
J.D. Tierney
Tim Tipton
Rodney Tisdale
Mary Todd
Elias Toldo
Loenel Toledo
Jack Tolleson
Fransisco Torres
Joel Torres
Juan Torres
Richard Trammel
Wayne Trammell
Donna Travis
Nathan Travis
Carlos Trejo
Reid Troxell
Ron Troxell
Anita Tryon
Beverly Tryon
Darrell Tryon
Rita Tryon
Scott Tryon
Tabitha Tryon
Tommy Tryon
Darin Turner
Marcus Turner
Grady Underwood
Tracy Upshaw
Justino Uriosugul
Tom Utz

Tracy Utz
Beverly Uzzell
Jerry Uzzell
Jose Luls Valdovinos
Brit Valentine
Maxima Valesquez
Jerry Vandergriff
Martin Vargas
Armando Vasquez
Isidro Vazquez
Vicente Vazquez
Angel Vega
Manuel Vela
Dan Velie
Sam Vercher
Manuel Villa
Daniel Viramontes
Ricardo Viramontes
Marcos Viveros
Eldridge Walker
Tim Walker
Barbara Wallace
Jason Wallace
Rick Wallop
Justin Wardlaw
Jason Wariner
John Wariner
Rodney Warren
Cindy Waterman
Eddy Waterman
Matthew Watson
Lee Weaver
Randy Weaver
Gary Welkel
Maggie Welkel
Phillip Welch
Jason Wellman
Steve Wells
Diane Welsh

John Wheless
Chris White
Derrick White
Randy Whitehead
Brenda Whiteley
Susan Wiggins
Tim Wiggins
Troy Wiggins
Don Wilburn
Troy Wildman
Amanda Williams
Jeremy Williams
Jessie Williams
Roy Williams
Corey Williamson
Judy Williamson
Jennifer Willis
John Willis
Joshua Wilson
Lisa Wilson
Randy Wilson
Scott Wilson
Barbara Winningham
Chris Woodall
Kim Woods
Weslee Worthington
Brenda Wright
Gus Wright
Lucio Yanez
John Yarbrough
Pat Yarbrough
William Yarbrough
Lori York
Mike York
Rudy Young
Shae Young
Andres Zavaleta
Victor Zin

"It's About Time..."

Finally, someone has produced a motivational presentation about a real success story and you and your company should see it! The "2 Hour House" documentary DVD has it all... teamwork, tension and triumph! Executive Producer, Brian Conaway, created this DVD as a unique motivational asset to businesses of any size. Not only do you get the full-length 60-minute documentary, but Conaway also includes a 20-minute snapshot version of the project, as well as a 3-minute music video featuring construction highlights, and a bonus 1 minute time-lapse of the construction!

More than simply building a house, this video provides excellent illustrations of extreme planning, critical path theory, timeline logistics, task delegation, value engineering, materials and labor coordination, all brought together under an intricate leadership structure. On October 1st, 2005, with Conaway's guidance as project leader, this group of hardworking volunteers built a 2249 square foot house, from the ground up in less than 3 hours... setting a new world record in home construction!

You get in-depth interviews from key team members, compelling narration that guides you through all phases of the project and unbelievable footage from five cameras shooting simultaneously.

If your company needs a supercharger to energize the next meeting — this DVD is it. Go behind the scenes of this amazing project to see how planning, team spirit, and hard work can accomplish the impossible!

- The 1-hour documentary takes you through the home-building project from its origin to the dramatic final moments before setting the new world record. Meet the men and women who made this project a reality, as they describe the excitement of about 1,000 skilled workers and volunteers dedicated to achieving a single goal.

- The 24-minute highlight video is a great motivational tool that groups and organizations can use to show teamwork and volunteerism.

- The 3-minute music video offers you a shorter review of the event's key moments.

- As a bonus, you also get a 1-minute time-lapse of this amazing project.

This DVD answers the question, "How on earth did they do that?"

www.2HourHouse.com